WOMEN of the WORD

This compilation copyright © BRF 2005

Published by
The Bible Reading Fellowship
First Floor, Elsfield Hall
15–17 Elsfield Way, Oxford OX2 8FG
Website: www.brf.org.uk

ISBN 1 84101 425 7
First published 2005
10 9 8 7 6 5 4 3 2 1 0
All rights reserved

A catalogue record for this book is available from the British Library

Printed by Gutenberg Press, Tarxien, Malta

WOMEN of the WORD

Discovering the women of the Bible

EDITED BY JACKIE STEAD

CONTRIBUTORS TO WOMEN OF THE WORD

Janet Evans is a freelance writer based in Kent.

Edna Hobbs ventures with God into various life situations, countries and denominations and is currently teaching in Dorset.

Anne Le Tissier is a devotional writer, actively supporting her husband in church ministry and spending some time working on retreats for people who are hurt, leading worship and providing prayer support.

Michele Morrison is a freelance writer based in Aberdeen.

Kristina Petersen works for Bible Reading Fellowship and as a freelance writer. She is a contributor to the Bible reading notes for women, *Day by Day with God*, and is based in Oxford.

Anne Roberts, who lives in Bolton, is a freelance writer and teaches in further and higher education.

CONTENTS

INTRODUCTION:
IT ALL BEGAN WITH TAMAR

To be honest, these Bible studies really started out as an indulgence for me. I had decided that it was time to read through the Bible again from beginning to end. I would be flexible—a few chapters one day, maybe a few verses the next; I would read until something 'spoke' to me and then I would note down the insights I learned.

My problem started early on—almost from the beginning and the story of Eve. What seemed to leap out at every turn was that women get a raw deal. It had not struck me so forcibly before, but suddenly I was indignant that Sarai should have to pretend that she was Abram's sister rather than his wife, appalled that Lot would sacrifice his daughters to the baying crowd, and angry at the misery in the lives of both Leah and Rachel because of their father's trickery. The final straw was the story of Judah and Tamar in Genesis 38.

Judah is the son of Jacob and Leah and, shortly after his younger brother Joseph is sold to the Midianites, he leaves his family and marries a Canaanite woman. They have three sons and Tamar becomes the wife of the eldest boy, whose name is Er.

Unfortunately Er is described as 'wicked in the Lord's sight' (v. 7) and is put to death rather quickly, so, as the custom of that time demanded, Judah's second son, Onan, is required to take Tamar as his wife and provide an heir for his brother. He is not keen on the idea and refuses to father the necessary child, so he too is put to death. Poor Tamar must now live as a widow in her father-in-law's house until the youngest son is old enough to marry her.

Years pass and it becomes clear that Judah is not going to keep his promise to give Tamar as a wife to his youngest son, so she has to take drastic action. She disguises herself and, mistaking her for a shrine prostitute, Judah asks her to sleep with him.

Three months later, Tamar's pregnancy is discovered and she is threatened with death. But Tamar had been clever. She could prove who the father was and is declared a righteous woman. She later gives birth to twin boys and there, it would seem, her story ends.

As I pondered the passage, I wondered what I was supposed to take from it. What was the point of it all? It simply seemed to typify the harsh life and injustice that faced many of the women in the Bible. I began to think about other women's stories in the Bible: surely I was missing something. I felt I wanted to understand them better.

I shared my thoughts with colleagues and with some of the women who had contributed Bible study features to *Woman Alive* in the past, and the response was very enthusiastic. We have now built up a team of writers who eagerly suggest ideas for the series, entitled 'Good Foundations', and then write the features that begin to unpack the women's stories in the Bible.

I must admit, I love receiving the articles each month; it's one of my favourite parts of the magazine to work on. We haven't tackled Tamar's story yet, but she has inspired the whole series. I have been moved, challenged, surprised and delighted as I have seen how the lives of these women reach down the centuries and speak into our lives today.

I hope these stories will speak to you, too.

Jackie Stead
Woman Alive

HAGAR: OUR GOD WHO SEES

BIBLE PASSAGE: GENESIS 16 AND 21

Hagar's story is, at first reading, a story of rejection and despair. But on closer inspection it is an illustration of the novelist Kurt Vonnegut's words: 'Unanticipated invitations to travel are dancing lessons with God.' Hagar was not so much invited as forced to travel, but behind the human hands that turned her out were the hands of a loving God, who had better things for her in the wilderness to which he lovingly drew her.

God had promised Abram that he would become a great nation, but his wife Sarai was childless, which was regarded as a mark of divine disfavour in the ancient world. This view is reflected in the Bible, though not having its origin there: it was a product of human anguish and need, of the human search for reasons to explain or explain away their difficulties, insisting on feeling that they have the answer to their 'Why'?

Legal provision was made for a wife's barrenness and what Sarai suggested was in accordance with that provision. She gave her slave girl Hagar to Abram to be his wife.

When Hagar became pregnant, she began to look down on Sarai, who passed the problem to Abram, turning it into a spiritual matter: 'The Lord decide between you and me!' (16:5). Abram, however, passed the buck straight back to Sarai. Legally, Sarai could not expel Hagar as she was now a wife in the household, so she got rid of the problem by making things so unpleasant for Hagar that she ran away.

What follows in Genesis 16 is a beautiful illustration of God's compassion for the forlorn and desolate, as Hagar receives an angelic visitation and has her first 'dancing lesson'. This outcast woman is the first person in the Bible to be visited by an angel. The phrase used here, 'the angel of the Lord' (v. 7) is sometimes used to denote God himself.

Hagar's attitude had not been helpful in a delicate situation, so to some extent we could say that she earned her banishment, but the visitor did not come with a rebuke about sin or self-pity or failure to remain steadfast in suffering. Instead, Hagar was addressed by name and gently asked, 'Where have you come from and where are you going?' (v. 8). God was concerned that Hagar should be where she and her unborn child could be provided for, so he told her to return to where she had come from. If she remained where she was, she would be destitute and subject to moral and physical dangers of an extreme kind.

God meets us where we are and, in treating us with compassion, leads us to repentance. The New Testament teaches us that God disciplines us for our good (Hebrews 12:10). We must learn to trust in his provision, no matter how contrary it may be to what we feel would comfort us.

But the angel didn't leave the situation like that. A slave girl, oppressed and dispossessed, was promised what only kings and chiefs would normally hope for: freedom. Hagar's son would be 'a wild ass of a man' (v. 12), implying someone who is not bound as a slave but is free to roam in the way of the Bedouin peoples, to whom a settled life is abhorrent. They make up their own minds, refusing to conform or to come under authority—hence the appearance of hostility in verse 12.

How hard it is when what we receive in life does not conform to our expectations! It takes time to discern God's provision. When we begin to do so, the dance becomes an interweaving of fear with faith, of encouragement with despair. We need God's Spirit to help us to continue in trust.

During a very traumatic time in my life, my faith in God did not waver but my feelings did not match that faith, and there were times when I plumbed depths of sadness that I did not know existed. Sometimes it would be after receiving a particularly unhelpful phone call or letter, to which my reactions were not always what they should have been; or I would just be sitting around doing nothing and going over in my mind what had taken place.

There was one such moment when I knew as never before that it is possible to know the immediate presence of God in the pit of despair, and to praise him simply because he is there. There were many times when, while I was actually weeping with grief, the phone would ring or a card would drop through the letterbox, or someone would arrive with a bunch of flowers. It was then that I knew beyond doubt that God had once again seen me and met my need.

Only recently, two years after the event that gave me such grief, I was very upset during a visit to friends by a conversation which stirred memories that should have been happy ones, but now could hold only sadness for me, because of what used to be and could be no more. Within ten minutes of our arriving home, a car drew up outside. Two friends who had been close to us in our grief had come to see us. We meet occasionally for dinner, but do not usually turn up at one another's door unannounced. They had come to bring a message from another friend who had supported us and whom they had met on holiday. God met my need for reassurance that, while I had lost so much, I had many treasures left which are beyond price.

Hagar's reaction, 'You are the God who sees me' (v. 13) , seems ordinary enough to us. We have the whole Bible to tell us that God sees! We have heard of and received his love for us in Jesus. Hagar, though, was used to being a second-class citizen. The last thing she would expect was God watching over her and responding to her need, implying that she mattered to him personally.

Even knowing what we know today, when we feel rejected or have experienced rejection, we can begin to suspect that it is some kind of withdrawal of God's hand on our lives. When we receive instances of God's seeing us, it is like a shaft of light in a very dark place.

Abram became Abraham and Sarai became Sarah. Hagar's son Ishmael was born, and all continued pleasantly enough until the son whom Sarah eventually bore, Isaac, began to grow into a lad. Ishmael began to taunt or tease the younger boy and Sarah saw danger. There must be no chance of her son's inheritance being shared with the son of a slave girl!

This time, God told Abraham to allow Sarah to do as she wished, assuring him that he would make Ishmael into a nation. So Abraham agreed that Hagar and Ishmael should leave (Genesis 21:13–14). As the water supply that they had taken with them ran out, Hagar received another angelic visitation, and her second 'dancing lesson' began. We are told that God heard the boy crying and came to her. He added to his earlier promise: this time the promise included that Ishmael would become a great nation—the same promise that he had made to Abraham for Isaac (Genesis 12:1–2). God's loving provision was then displayed in that Hagar found herself to be in a place where there was a well.

So Hagar, the lone parent, moved into her desert wanderings. It cannot have been easy for her to imagine or actually hear of God blessing and prospering those she had left, when they had treated her so harshly. I hope she was able to let go of the past and forgive them.

This is particularly hard to do when those who have hurt us do not recognize it or repent of it. If we accept that God forgives us even our worst sins, though, we must accept that he does the same for others and that we must try to do so as well. We can only leave their lack of repentance with him and try to say with Jesus, 'Father, forgive them, for they do not know what they are doing' (Luke 23:34). Perhaps they do know, perhaps they don't, but our hanging on to the offence will not help us or God's work in our lives.

I like to imagine Hagar in later life, climbing a hill overlooking her son's desert territory and watching the activity in the camp below. She has the evidence before her of her son's prosperity in family, household, livestock, household goods and who knows what other treasures. She watches her grandchildren at play and considers the life she would have had with Abraham and Sarah, always coming second to Sarah, with Ishmael second to Isaac, who would be heir to Abraham's wealth. Here, she is matriarch and her son patriarch. She knows that she is in the better place, the place of God's provision.

So many of us have come out of a situation, a relationship, a church or a job where once we felt secure and happy. The uprooting was painful, seemingly beyond endurance, but we can know now that the seeing and hearing God was in it all. He saw our predicament. He saw where we were at fault and where others were, but he opened up his arms of love to us and to them and took us on to better things. Perhaps angels ministered to us!

Reflect

- Have you ever been mistreated? How did you react? Have you laid it all at God's feet and come to thank him for his provision?
- When did you know in a special way that God was seeing your situation?

✢

Prayer

Lord God, during those times when your ways with us seem harsh, help us to be still and trust in your wisdom. You do know the end from the beginning. You have given us a future and a hope. Grant us your peace, dear Father.

ANNE ROBERTS

RAHAB: A HEROINE OF THE FAITH

BIBLE PASSAGE: JOSHUA 2 AND 6

The latter rains had dispersed, but an ominous cloud continued to threaten Canaan. The shadow of death cast gloom over the land in which Jericho lay in vulnerable anticipation. Reports of the Amorites' annihilation, east of the Jordan, had paralysed their hearts with unabashed fear.

Squatting among piles of drying flax, Rahab seized a quiet moment to contemplate her situation. Building up her 'business' had been a life's work but, like the fading blue petals scattered across the floor, her future was now looking fragile.

Anxious, she sought solace in material facts. The Israelites were on the banks of the river, but only the toughest of men could possibly cross that swollen death-trap at this time of year. Furthermore, the strength and resilience of the city's immense casement walls made them impenetrable. Some 3.5 metres thick, they were further fortified by homes built into their inward side, her own included. The soldiers atop the wall were well armed for battle, so surely those Israelite shepherds couldn't make any impact with their limited artillery?

For Jericho's security to be threatened by ill-equipped desert nomads, its fear of this rabble must spring from some awesome power, veiled from sight behind their inadequate appearance. With this realization, God awakened Rahab's soul to the truth, enticing her to transfer allegiance from her old gods and masters.

Her thoughts were interrupted by a knock at the hostel door. Her bright eyes darted across weatherworn faces as two travellers asked for a bed. Tradesmen were regular visitors, but only years in the desert could have manufactured that leathery skin; she could have stretched it over a drum! Her poignant questions amazed the spies, but their biggest surprise unfolded with her timely assistance as another knock battered the door.

She was shrewd, and well prepared for the king's messengers, securing their trust with feigned sincerity: 'Yes, the men came to me, but I did not know where they had come from. At dusk, when it was time to close the city gate, the men left. I don't know which way they went. Go after them quickly. You may catch up with them' (Joshua 2:4–5).

Back on the roof, flax stalks parted like hair and vivid eyes peered out at her from within. Divulging the great fear that had fallen upon the city, she spoke of the Israelites' flight from Egypt and the recent obliteration of Sihon and Og. With mounting fervour, she testified to her faith in their God, humbly entreating them for her life and family.

'"Our lives for your lives!" the men assured her. "If you don't tell what we are doing, we will treat you kindly and faithfully when the Lord gives us the land"' (v. 14).

The scarlet cord lifted gently in the breeze, a secret 'au revoir' to her lithe conspirators, 'until we meet again'.

Despite her Canaanite birth and ungodly lifestyle, Rahab is included in the 'hall of fame' in the book of Hebrews as a heroine of faith, the only woman to be so named (Hebrews 11:31). She listened to reports of God, responded to what she heard, believed and put her faith into action, a faith that has been commended ever since. What can we learn from her example?

Faith that acts

'A person is justified by what he does and not by faith alone. In the same way, was not even Rahab the prostitute considered righteous for what she did when she gave lodging to the spies and sent them off in a different direction?' (James 2:24–25).

What is faith? 'Faith is being sure of what we hope for and certain of what we do not see' (Hebrews 11:1). When we have this depth of assurance, it's not merely an intellectual belief, but a conviction that manifests itself in all aspects of life. Faith expresses itself in deeds. God looks further than a person's belief in his existence; after all, even the demons believe that! (James 2:19). Faith and deeds work hand-in-hand, a seamless entity and therefore inseparable: 'faith by itself, if it is not accompanied by action, is dead' (James 2:17).

If Rahab had merely told the spies that she believed in their God, but did nothing to hide or help them, her statement would have tumbled with the walls of Jericho. Likewise, actions validate the sincerity of our profession of faith. Good, religious deeds won't save us—only God's mercy and our rebirth through Jesus Christ can do so—but the acceptance of God's gift of grace is proved in action.

Faith that bears testimony

'Joshua spared Rahab the prostitute, with her family and all who belonged to her' (Joshua 6:25).

In order for Rahab's father, mother, brothers and all who belonged to her to be saved from death, they had to be in her house when the Israelites attacked. Rahab needed a good reason to dissuade them from joining the ranks atop the wall. What could be better than her personal testimony? Once again, she put her life at risk, for they could have rejected her, proclaimed her insane and told the authorities. She was desperate for them to be saved, however, so she trusted God, and shared her faith.

Faith that trusts in all circumstances

'Now Jericho was tightly shut up because of the Israelites. No one went out and no one came in' (Joshua 6:1).

Any scrap of courage in Jericho must have vanished the day the Israelites crossed the Jordan on dry ground (Joshua 5:1). Rahab was cornered, with no idea how the spies' oath could be honoured —her only reminder, a flimsy scarlet cord.

Leaning not on her own understanding, she trusted God for his answer. Until then, she lived as best she could under the circumstances. Death crept forward like the incoming tide, each wave inching closer to its prey. The tension mounted, she received no comforting news, but still she waited. God answered in his perfect time and the scarlet cord continued to fly on the pinnacle of stone that towered above Jericho's devastation.

The scarlet thread of redemption weaves itself through history. The Passover blood on the doorposts, the cord in the window, the blood shed on the cross; each identifies a means of salvation, a redemptive cloak of righteousness for the sinner who trusts in a holy God.

Faith fully immersed in God's holy code of life

'And she lives among the Israelites to this day' (Joshua 6:25b). Rahab was first placed outside the Israelite camp (6:23), but later lived 'among' them and therefore had to be naturalized. This meant accepting the code of life demanded and regulated by God's law, something quite alien to her former culture but which made her faith a daily, living reality. She is named in the genealogy of Jesus for giving birth to Salmon's son Boaz, David's great-grandfather (Matthew 1:5). Assuming that this is the same Rahab, it is evidence of her complete integration within God's people and purposes. Turning her back on the smouldering heap of her past, Rahab walked into the promised land, learning, adapting and submitting to a new code of behaviour.

God hates lukewarm attention (Revelation 3:16). Lot's wife looked back and became a pillar of salt (Genesis 19:26). Rahab's contemporaries didn't act on the reports, and turned into dust. We can't take any mementos from our 'Jericho' to remind us of the past. We have to turn our back, and walk away.

The holy code of life that we find in the word of God is perfectly exemplified through our Saviour Jesus Christ. God doesn't want us to live outside his camp, just dipping in here and there as we see fit. He expects full immersion. His grace isn't a licence to keep sinning, but teaches us to subdue our worldly passions and live self-controlled, upright and godly lives (Titus 2:11–12).

The Bible applauds Rahab, not for righteous behaviour but for faith proved by deeds. She isn't a plumb-line against which to measure our righteousness, for we all fall short of Christ's perfect lifestyle, but here's a challenge from a fellow sinner to love God with all that we are, trust God with everything we have, and revere God as we work out our salvation.

Reflect

* Rahab's act of faith advanced God's kingdom on earth. God gives us the gift of faith for his glory. Are we advancing his kingdom, or is our faith merely an insurance policy, friendship club or help centre? (See Ephesians 2:10; Philippians 2:12–13.)
* Not every story shares this happy ending, but how desperate are we, and to what extent are we prepared to go, to share our testimony—what we're doing for God and what he's doing for us—with non-believing family members and friends? (See 1 Peter 3:15; Revelation 12:11.)
* When faith is tested through adversity, our cravings for immediate answers, comfort or satisfaction may reach out for something tangible that isn't necessarily of God. Where have we put our trust today? Who is our comfort and guide? (See Galatians 5:7; Hebrews 12:1.)
* Have we completely taken off our former way of life and donned the new self that is created to be like God, or has God's Spirit

pinpointed a rebellious streak that needs to submit to the cross?
(See Ephesians 4:22–24; Romans 6:19–23.)

✤

Prayer

*Thank you, Lord, for using anyone in your kingdom work, not just the
'super-spiritual'. Show me how my faith can play its part in serving
you, and teach me your ways, that I may reflect Jesus in my everyday
life. Amen.*

ANNE LE TISSIER

RUTH: WHERE YOU GO, I WILL GO

BIBLE PASSAGE: THE BOOK OF RUTH

Ruth was born in Moab, a pariah of a country polluted with the worship of vile gods who craved child sacrifices. She met the living God in the home of her husband, Mahlon, a refugee from the famine in Israel. Mahlon's father Elimelech had died shortly after the move to Moab, and Mahlon and his brother Kilion settled down with their mother Naomi and married local girls.

Both Moabitesses loved Naomi. When Mahlon and Kilion died, and Naomi headed home, Ruth and Orpah started out with her. Their decision to accompany their mother-in-law to a country often at war with their own nation was a costly one. Without social security or insurance policies, and bereft of their husbands, Orpah and Ruth were walking away from the help available to them in Moab. Each had a family home to which they could return, offering security, shelter, food, and hope for a normal future. Nothing like that waited for them in Israel. Naomi was old, Israel was a dark unknown and, as three women alone, they were destitute.

No doubt such thoughts agitated Orpah's mind as she trudged towards Bethlehem alongside a bitter Naomi. For ten years she had lived with Naomi, who offers one of the Bible's earliest examples of relational evangelism. She loved her mother-in-law. She was attracted by the light of God in her, but her focus rested on the human Naomi and not the divine spark that inspired her. She trusted Naomi, but that was not enough. For such a sacrifice, she needed to trust in God.

There are people like Orpah, who hang around Christians,

clustering on the fringe of the church. But, when a situation arises that demands tough obedience and sacrifice, they fall back. They return to their substandard comfort zones rather than stepping forward into the unknown, trusting in God.

One of the dangers of relational evangelism is that people can attribute the godly traits they see in Christians to natural human characteristics, and fail to see the true source of those traits.

Ruth, however, knew God. 'Where you go I will go, and where you stay, I will stay. Your people will be my people and your God my God,' she declared to Naomi (Ruth 1:16). She was not inspired by a desire to help an old woman; she was inspired by God. He was her hope, and God, who yearns for the lost, never disappoints. Ruth's commitment must have delighted his heart.

How often do we fail to delight our God who loves us, because we rely on the 'seen' rather than trusting in his bountiful goodness and mercy? We have a lot of safety nets and, until they all give way and we land in God's everlasting arms, we trust in them. Orpah fell back into the darkness of Moab but, in a breathtaking act of faith, Ruth stepped forward into (from a human standpoint) a dangerous unknown, putting her faith in God and walking into the light.

In her only assertion of independence, Ruth rejected Naomi's instruction to return to her mother's home. She had met the living God, and she chose to shelter under the shadow of his wings. She shrugged off the security of her mother's home, the familiarity of Moabite life and, arm-in-arm with Naomi, headed north-west.

Jesus said, 'No one who puts his hand to the plough and looks back is fit for service in the kingdom of God' (Luke 9:62). Orpah looked back, but Ruth didn't. Ruth responded to God's call on her life. By her actions she demonstrated that it is more important to live in God's will than to live in any particular locality. It is the same for us. To fail to move forward where God is calling us, to choose to stay behind in what common sense says is a 'safe place', is to miss a great blessing.

Is God calling you to move on somewhere that appears hazardous? Is he calling me? May we all respond with the risk-taking faith of Ruth! Stepping out of our comfort zone is scary, and Ruth appreciated the risks. Can you not hear the desperation in Ruth's plea to Naomi, 'Don't urge me to leave you or to turn back from you' (1:16)? The decision wasn't easy for her, despite her faith, but she 'was determined to go with' Naomi (1:18).

Following God doesn't mean abandoning clear thinking and common sense. When they arrived in Israel, Ruth didn't sit back and do nothing. She was a healthy young woman, and she showed her willingness to work hard by going out to glean behind the harvesters. She scavenged for their survival. Having gained Naomi's permission (which may reveal more than respectful obedience: Ruth sought practical advice as she was in a foreign land with foreign customs), she worked 'steadily from morning... except for a short rest in the shelter' (2:7).

Day after day, Ruth went out into the fields and gleaned. Perhaps her fortitude and love restored Naomi's own shaken faith, for as the harvest continued and neared its conclusion, Naomi made a suggestion. She thought of Boaz, a relative, and advised Ruth to take steps (which seem alien to us and were certainly hazardous) to secure their future—and a secure future for women in that society meant a husband.

It may seem that Naomi was a scheming matchmaker, but surely God was behind this match. It was more than a coincidence that Ruth found herself working in the fields of Boaz. It was one of those 'God-incidences'.

We have a custom in our home of keeping Christmas cards in a basket and, every morning during the following year, pulling one out and praying for those who sent it. The choice of card is apparently random, as we dive in and just pull one out. It seems haphazard, but it isn't, for in response to our short notes informing people of our prayers for them that day, we frequently hear back that on that particular day, prayers were particularly needed. There might be a new pregnancy, crumbling family circumstances, holiday traumas. We heard from a dear friend who asked, incredulously, if we'd known that that day was her 93rd birthday. We hadn't—but

God had! God is in charge of the little and the large things in life. Nothing is left to chance.

God had wonderful plans for Ruth, who lived a humble, obedient and godly life by the light she'd been given. She worked diligently and shared everything she gathered or was given with her mother-in-law. She approached Boaz with respect and deference and, though she was in a very vulnerable position humanly speaking, she was safe, sheltering under God's wing.

God was bowled over by her faith. Centuries later, Jesus was equally bowled over by the faith of another Gentile, a Roman centurion, and exclaimed, 'I have not found such great faith even in Israel' (Luke 7:9). Is he bowled over by your faith, or by mine?

When I married Don and moved to Scotland, I was terribly homesick for California. Often I recalled the words of the poem by John Keats, 'Ode to a Nightingale', in which he speaks of 'the sad heart of Ruth, when, sick for home/She stood in tears amid the alien corn'. Ruth has been my inspiration over these many years, because although she may have longed for home, she longed for God even more. Hard though it was, she chose to cling to God. He loved that risk-taking, sacrificial love and blessed her abundantly.

Yes, I love Ruth. Spiritually she was on the journey with God, and that inspired her every move. God loved her courage and her perseverance, and he rewarded it. Women may have counted for nothing in that society, but not in God's book, for it is Ruth's name that is linked with David's and Jesus' in Matthew 1, not Elimelech's or Mahlon's. Ruth, the Moabitess, is listed in the genealogy of the Son of God. Amazing!

Nobody is excluded from God's kingdom because of background or nationality: it is by faith that we are saved. Ruth demonstrated extraordinary faith in the God of Israel and he honoured the trust she put in him. He gave her a son by her husband Boaz, and that little boy, Obed, became the grandfather of David, the great king of Israel.

May we all love God with the total abandonment that Ruth showed, and walk with him wherever he leads us.

Reflect

- How resolute is my faith? Is my soul clinging to the Lord? (Psalm 63:8).
- How committed am I to praying for the Naomis of today, believers who quietly follow Jesus while living in dark countries where other gods reign?

✛

Prayer

Lord, give me a heart overflowing with love for you, that I may live a life of abandonment, sold out to you for ever. Amen.
MICHELE MORRISON

NAOMI: WHEN HOPE SEEMS GONE

BIBLE PASSAGE: THE BOOK OF RUTH

Hope. It is one of three things that will remain, Paul tells us in 1 Corinthians 13:13, along with faith and love. Most of us would wholeheartedly agree to the importance of the eternal nature of faith and love. How could we live without our faith and the assurance that at least God loves us, even if nobody else does? It doesn't bear thinking about! But hope? Being reasonably young and optimistic by nature, I had always taken hope for granted, until recently.

Even on a bad day, or when difficulties arose, I always expected that winter would turn to summer, sadness to joy. For me, hope had always been intricately woven with faith and love, unseen and perhaps a little unappreciated. But when my husband died, I discovered the importance of hope. The sure hope that Alan was now with Jesus and that God had a good plan for my life gave me the strength to keep living.

My difficulties are small compared to the afflictions of some. Consider Naomi's tragedy: a refugee in a foreign land, it seemed that everything precious to her was stripped away. Praise God, there was a happy ending, but first Naomi had to go through much suffering, as we read in the book of Ruth.

Naomi's difficulties started in Bethlehem, where she lived with her husband Elimelech and their two sons. There was a famine in the land, so the family left Bethlehem and went to Moab, where they had heard there was food. In Moab, disaster struck. First, Elimelech died. The two sons married Moabite girls, but after a little while the boys also died. There weren't even any grand-children to help to ease Naomi's pain. Few of us, I guess, can imagine the depth of her grief.

No wonder, as she said in her own words, Naomi felt bitter (Ruth 1:20). Often in Bible studies, we compare this poor, sad widow unfavourably with Ruth, her kind and selfless daughter-in-law. But maybe we should not be too harsh on Naomi. Would your heart not go out to an elderly refugee who had lost not only her husband but also both her sons?

I have not lost either of my boys, so I cannot begin to imagine how much that must hurt, but there are hardly words to express the pain of the loss of my husband. For Naomi to lose the whole of her family must have been almost more than she could bear. Yet, in all her grief, it seemed that she held on to hope. Having heard that barley was once again being harvested in Bethlehem, Naomi decided to leave Moab and return to her people and her God. She could not have made a better decision.

It may well have been a mistake to have left Bethlehem in the first place. Naomi was living in the times of the Judges, when it is said that 'every man did what was right in his own eyes' (Judges 21:25, RSV). Perhaps Elimelech and his sons were doing what was right in their own eyes, rather than relying on God.

It is tempting, when there seems to be famine among the Lord's people, to move away and feed ourselves from another source. Grass may look greener on the other side, but it is usually a trick of the shadows; there may be short-term satisfaction elsewhere, but in the end running away can only bring pain.

If you are considering leaving, be absolutely certain that you are doing the right thing. It is easy to blame God or his people (particularly church leaders!) for our lack of nourishment, but we should never rely on others alone. We may long for showers of blessing, but during times of drought we must reach our own roots down deeper, where the water table may have dropped but water still runs fresh, clear and abundant.

Perhaps God is withholding the harvest due to church family or even national disobedience. Perhaps we are part of the problem, perhaps not; either way, our prayers, presence and encouragement are needed. When times are hard, we need to get on our knees and pray for forgiveness, love and mercy, not run away like spoilt children.

If you should find yourself far from God's blessing, however, follow Naomi's example and go home. Return to God and to his people, where there is forgiveness and hope for the future. The journey back may cause you pain. You may also have to face people on your return and admit to hurts and failures, but it will be worth it.

Naomi's journey home must have been miserable. No Orient Express links Moab to Bethlehem! She probably had to travel in a camel train, sleeping rough, feeling old and weary, perhaps with aching joints and sore feet. There was the sad memory of the outward journey with her family to contend with, and she must have dreaded facing the neighbours again, imagining their reaction to her misfortune, especially in a culture where it would be seen as God's curse to have no one to carry on the family name.

No doubt some neighbours were sympathetic, but some would say, 'I told you so.' Some would whisper behind her back, while some would unthinkingly show off how their own grandchildren had grown. God's people are not perfect yet. Naomi must have gone over so many times in her mind her speech to the people of Bethlehem on her return: 'Don't call me Naomi [which means pleasant]. Call me Mara [which means bitter]' (Ruth 1:20).

But thank God that he loves widows, the hungry, and all who are needy, weary and bowed low with heavy burdens. So God sent Ruth to Naomi, to care for her in her distress. At first, Naomi tried to persuade Ruth to stay in Moab with her family, but Ruth insisted on accompanying her mother-in-law back to Bethlehem. How grateful Naomi must have been!

We all need a Ruth from time to time—someone sent by God to help us through trying times. Whether they be friends or family, one person or several, foreigner or even mother-in-law, we all need people who will never leave us, even when we are rotten company, crushed by grief and perhaps bitter at what life has dealt us. Don't let's turn them away!

Back in Bethlehem, it was not long before Naomi acknowledged God's gracious hand once more at work in her life. Ruth went out in the fields to glean grain for food, returning triumphantly on the first day with plenty of barley and tales of the kindness of Boaz, a generous and godly man in whose field she had worked. Naomi surely must have smiled, perhaps for the first time in many months, for not only was there food to eat, but Boaz was a close relative.

Encouraged, she made a very unselfish decision. Putting her own needs aside, she decided to work for Ruth's happiness and do a bit of matchmaking.

Now, your 'Ruth' may not appreciate your organizing her a husband! But when you can, lift your head again from your pain, leave 'Bitter' behind and become 'Pleasant' again, for everybody else's sake as much as your own. Don't imprison yourself in bitterness. It is fine to accept help while you need it, but give, too, when you are able. There is a time to weep and a time to mourn, as the writer of Ecclesiastes tells us, but he also notes that there is a time to laugh and a time to dance (Ecclesiastes 3:4). I know this is true; I have joined a salsa class!

As in the most satisfying of stories, everything turned out beautifully for Naomi in the end. As Jesus did for us, Boaz redeemed all that was hers. Ruth married Boaz and together they had a son, Obed. Naomi lost everything in Moab, but from the ashes of mourning rose the joy of new birth—a beautiful grandson. I wonder what Naomi felt when she held Obed for the first time. Among many emotions, surely there was hope for the future. Because of the sin in this world, all of our lives are going to be a mixture of pain and pleasure, sadness and joy. But if we trust in God, we can always be assured that, along with faith and love, our hope will remain for ever.

Reflect

- What are you hoping for?
- Do you put your hope in God or in your circumstances?
- Thank God that the hope that he gives is absolutely certain and will last for ever.

✤

Prayer

Thank you so much, dear Father, for the people you have sent to help me in times of need. Help me to trust in you always, accept help graciously when I need it, and bless others when I am able. Amen.
JANET EVANS

ABIGAIL: WOMAN OF WISDOM

BIBLE PASSAGE: 1 SAMUEL 25:2–35

Abigail is seldom listed among the 'celebrity' women of the Bible, Sarah, Ruth, Esther and Mary, along with 'Proverbs 31 woman', being the usual paragons held up to us. Yet it was Abigail who taught David the lesson that influenced him most, and that is one of the most important lessons we will ever learn.

Her story begins in 1 Samuel 25:2 and is chiefly told by verse 35, although we catch glimpses of her again in 1 Samuel 30:5–18, 2 Samuel 3:3 and 1 Chronicles 3:1. A mere woman at a time when women were viewed as no more than a man's possessions, Abigail had the misfortune to be married to Nabal, whose name literally means 'fool'. The Bible does not mince its words about this arrogant brute: his lack of wisdom is commented on many times and referred to by several people. Abigail, on the other hand, is described as intelligent and good-looking (v. 3), and when the servants are appalled by their master's stupidity they turn to her to remedy the dire situation.

In the days when David was on the run from Saul, he lived in bandit country with a following of about 600 fighting men and their dependants. During this time, David was learning to trust God for his very existence. Living in desert hideouts and trying to elude a Saul determined to hunt him down, he not only had his and his men's safety to worry about, he also had to feed them.

When David heard that the prosperous Nabal was shearing sheep, he knew there would be a feast for all the shepherds gathered there, so he sent ten young men to ask whether the fugitive band could join in. Earlier, when these same shepherds had been grazing their sheep in the dangerous wilderness, David and his band had protected them from attack by roving raiders.

David's request was extremely polite—'Give whatever your heart tells you to your servants and to me, David, your son' (v. 8, *THE MESSAGE*)—but Nabal's response was contemptuous and provoked David to vow that by the following morning Nabal and his household would be slaughtered for his ingratitude.

Anticipating David's response to his master's unfairness, one of Nabal's servants had the foresight to let Abigail know what was going on. 'Do something quickly because big trouble is ahead for our master and us,' wailed the shepherd (v. 17, *THE MESSAGE*). *THE MESSAGE* translates the next verse as 'Abigail flew into action' (v. 18).

No, she didn't tell Nabal what an arrogant idiot he'd been, nor did she try to make him realize just what disaster he'd called down upon them by his meanness: Abigail dashed about preparing a feast as a peace offering to David. The Bible records in detail what she prepared to take to him, to show that her response was a generous one: she was not making a gesture to fob David off; she was compensating for her husband's rudeness to him. To underscore that, she doesn't send the feast to David, but takes it to him herself.

David was on his way to kill the household when he and Abigail met in a ravine. She fell on her knees in homage, apologizing and explaining that she'd not been there to hear his request. She approached David with an appeasing and conciliatory attitude. Nonetheless, she was not debasing herself; she knew exactly what she was doing—her strength and not her fear made her kneel before David.

'Forgive my presumption,' said Abigail (v. 24, *THE MESSAGE*) and then reminded David that God had a plan for his life, a plan that did not include egotistical responses. David had felt insulted that doing the right thing by Nabal had not brought the deserved gratitude: without challenging David directly about his macho tantrum, Abigail reminded him that vengeance belongs to God with these wonderful words: 'Know this: Your God-honoured life is tightly bound in the bundle of God-protected life; but the lives of your enemies will be hurled aside as a stone is thrown from a sling' (v. 29, THE MESSAGE).

Abigail prevented David from having Nabal's blood on his hands: 'When God completes all the goodness he has promised my master and sets you up as prince over Israel, my master will not have this dead weight in his heart, the guilt of an avenging murder' (v. 31, THE MESSAGE).

David thanked Abigail, accepted her other gifts and promised not to harm Nabal's household, but to leave it to God to sort out. One of the characteristics that made sinful David 'a man after God's own heart' (1 Samuel 13:14) was that very reliance on God to sort matters out and his willingness to listen to the messengers God sent to him to pull him back on track.

When Abigail got home, she found Nabal very drunk (v. 36). How tempting it must have been to lash out and let him know what a fool he was. What a chance to pour out scorn and contempt on the disgusting brute—but she took her own advice and left it to God. In the morning, when Nabal was sober, she told him what she had done and how David had turned from his revenge. Nabal got such a fright that he had a heart attack and, after being in a coma for ten days, he died.

The lessons we can learn from Abigail fall into two categories: what she teaches us unwittingly through her behaviour, and the lesson she set out to share with David. Abigail is an important role model, especially for those of us who cringe from a 'goody-goody doormat' image.

- She showed initiative, deciding how to solve a problem and wasting no time in getting on with it.
- She was very brave, venturing off on her donkey to find 600 angry men.
- She had a sense of self-worth: when she talked of her 'gift' (v. 27), she was not only referring to the food, she was alluding to the 'reminder' she proceeded to give David.

- She wasn't afraid to accept help herself: 'And when God has worked things for good for my master, remember me' (v. 31, *THE MESSAGE*).

We all have unreasonable, pig-headed idiots in authority over us at some time or other in our lives, and Abigail gives us a model for dealing with them:

- Focus on what needs to be done; don't bother spitting fury.
- Compensate for their blunders generously, leaving God to deal with them.
- When the time is right, inform them of your solutions but don't bring up their failings.

It is always tricky trying to point out destructive behaviour to someone and help them back on track: often we end up doing more harm than good. Abigail's example when she met David was a guide to a non-confrontational encounter.

- A humble, submissive approach is not a weak one, it is a calming one; when we kneel first, we kneel in strength. Make sure you kneel before you presume to teach!
- Refocus attention on God's promises and desires rather than spelling out where others have strayed from his plan.
- When you've done what God sent you to do, be quiet, go away and wait for God to work; then respond promptly when you're called.

Those are some of the lessons that we can learn through observing Abigail, but the lesson that David grasped when Abigail spoke to him is what we need to learn most: when we are living in God, he will deal with those who seek to harm us. He will make sure that their plans are thwarted, that any hurt inflicted is transformed to ultimate good and that they do not triumph over us in the long term.

Having learnt that lesson, David could leave a sleeping Saul to

God's vengeance, though he was close enough to slit his throat (1 Samuel 26:9–12). In fact, he could receive from his enemy, Saul himself, a blessing: 'Succeed in all you attempt' (26:25, THE MESSAGE).

Abigail's name means 'father (that is, cause or source) of joy/delight'. If we learn the lesson she taught David, we too will have cause for joy and will be a source of delight to God. So with David we can say to Abigail: 'Blessed be the Lord God of Israel, who sent you this day to meet me! And blessed is your advice and blessed are you, because you have kept me this day from coming to bloodshed and avenging myself with my own hand' (25:32–33, NKJ).

Take Abigail's advice: let God fight your battles.

Reflect

• If I have given my life to God, why don't I trust him to look after me, to deal with those who seek to harm me? Doesn't God know best how to pay them back? And actually, don't I really want more than that: wouldn't a blessing from those who've tried to curse me be the best outcome of all?

✠

Prayer

Lord God and Father of us all, keep me from petty human squabbles. Keep my eyes on you and your intentions for me. Take away that element of ego that makes me want to show others how awful or mistaken they are. Help me to leave you to sort out my enemies; help me to trust you to transform their curse into a blessing. Thank you that I can now cast this care on you, knowing that through Jesus I am set free of all my burdens, guilt and worries. Amen.

EDNA HOBBS

THE UNNAMED SERVANT GIRL: IMPORTANT IN GOD'S EYES

BIBLE PASSAGE: 2 KINGS 5

She had been abducted, taken away from her family, familiar surroundings and all she held dear. She had been taken to an alien place, to people she didn't know, and was made to work for them. She knew that she would never see her home town, her family, her people again. She was a servant, a slave with no rights, no choices and no influence. She had every reason to be bitter towards those foreigners who had taken her captive and deprived her of her future. But she wasn't.

I am talking about the girl referred to in 2 Kings 5. Her name is not even mentioned and what it says in these two verses is all we know about her: 'Now bands from Aram had gone out and had taken captive a young girl from Israel, and she served Naaman's wife. She said to her mistress, "If only my master would see the prophet who is in Samaria! He would cure him of his leprosy"' (vv. 2–3).

Naaman is a man of influence. He is commander of the army of Aram (Syria) and is well-regarded because he has won a battle (probably the battle against Israel mentioned in 1 Kings 22)—or, as it says in 2 Kings 5:1, 'through him the Lord had given victory to Aram'. It is unlikely that Naaman would have acknowledged the Lord at this point. Naaman also has a skin disease that makes him ritually unclean.

Why should the unnamed servant girl care about Naaman, even

feel sorry for him? After all, she is the one who is far from home, someone to be pitied. He is an important man who, we can assume, has doctors at his disposal. Yet she does care, enough to mention to Naaman's wife that there is a prophet who could help Naaman. The girl may live in captivity but she has not forgotten her faith.

Her casual remark has consequences. Naaman's wife takes the insignificant servant seriously. Maybe she recognizes the wisdom and faith in this foreign girl. Maybe here are two women who, despite being in completely different circumstances, understand each other.

Naaman's wife (again, a woman who is not named) must have told her husband about the remarks of the servant girl, for the next thing we know is that Naaman talks to the king of Aram, who tells him to go. Interestingly, the king doesn't send him to the prophet but to the king of Israel, laden with gifts, as if healing can be bought.

The king of Israel (not named, but probably Jehoram) is rather frightened by the whole affair. He's faced with a commander of a foreign army bearing rather over-the-top gifts and asking him to 'play God' and cure someone of leprosy (or another skin disease: the term was used for all sorts of unsightly skin diseases). The king doesn't think of praying to God or of consulting the prophet.

Enter Elisha, the prophet. He tells the king to send Naaman to him so that he can sort him out, but then Elisha just sends a messenger to Naaman to tell him what to do. Naaman's pride is hurt and he is not pleased. He doesn't want to wash in the river Jordan; there are better rivers at home, thank you very much. He wants the prophet to do something spectacular!

Once again it is the seemingly insignificant that solves the problem: Naaman's servants persuade him to wash in the river Jordan, as instructed. Naaman is healed of his skin disease but he gains much more than that. He realizes and acknowledges that 'there is no God in all the world except in Israel' (v. 15). He comes to faith, and 'his flesh was restored and became clean like that of a young boy' (v. 14). The word used in Hebrew for 'boy' is the masculine form of the word used for the servant girl in verses 2 and 3. By listening to his servants and swallowing his pride, Naaman gains something that the girl serving his wife has had all along: faith in the only true God, the God of Israel.

An example for us

The servant girl, probably still young, could have felt very angry at her situation. She might have had a happy life in Israel, among her own people. Maybe she had dreamt of getting married and having a family of her own: that was what her future back in Israel would most probably have held for her. Now all this had been taken away from her, for good. Why had the God she worshipped allowed this to happen? Why was she in this situation? Why did she have to serve the wife of a commander who had defeated the army of her people?

This girl sets an example for us all by not asking the question, 'What if... had happened?', by not looking back to a past she has lost, by not blaming other people or God for her misfortune. She serves her mistress and their relationship is obviously good enough for them to have the conversation that changes Naaman's life. She loves those whom she could have considered her enemies. She cares enough for Naaman to want him to be healed. Little does she know that God will use her good heart for his purposes.

Naaman thought he was so important that the prophet should surely come out to him and wave his arms around and arrange for some great miracle. Just washing in a river didn't seem grand enough for this grand man. He does see sense in the end, though, because he listens to his servants, those of seemingly little influence. Then he wants to pay for the miracle of his healing, but Elisha won't have it. Healing, both of body and mind, is free—a gift from God that cannot be bought. It is free for us, too. We cannot buy healing; we cannot bribe God into doing anything for us. It is a free gift and that can be hard to accept.

We are important in God's eyes

Do you ever feel insignificant? Do you ever feel that you have no influence, maybe not even many choices—that what you think doesn't matter? Do you sometimes long to do something big for God but don't know where to start? Yes, me too! This story can encourage us. God's economy is different and those who are insignificant in the world's eyes can be used as powerfully by God as any king or ruler, any politician or leader or boardroom member.

All the girl did was hold on to her faith and her integrity in adverse circumstances. She cared for those around her because she realized that they, too, were fragile human beings in need of God. She could see that behind the outward appearance of an influential army commander, with servants to look after him and on good terms with the king, was a man in need of God's touch.

Think about the people you know personally and the people you read about in the paper or see on TV. They may seem important, so much more important than you and me. They may even think so themselves. In God's eyes, however, each one of us is as important as any of those in influential positions.

Women have often been in the background and have influenced situations from there, sometimes without realizing it. Don't ever think that you can do nothing and that you are not important. You are important to God and that is all that matters. He can use you, he can use me—just as he used the servant girl.

P.S. The story doesn't end here. Read 2 Kings 5:19–27 to find out what happened to Gehazi, Elisha's servant, as the result of Naaman's coming to Elisha. Gehazi was rather greedy and it all ended in tears for him. The servant girl's remark even had consequences for him.

Reflect

- Do you ever neglect to do something positive because you think it is insignificant and doesn't matter? Think back to times when a remark or small gesture by someone else had great influence on your own life or the life of someone you know.
- Do you hold a grudge against someone? Do you like to think back fondly to a time in the past when life seemed better? Sit down now and give this person or situation to God. Resolve to let go of the person or situation into God's hand gradually, over the next few days, weeks or months.

❖

Prayer

Lord God, thank you that I am a royal diadem in your hand (Isaiah 62:3) and of infinite value to you. Please help me to be open to your voice, and please use me in both small and great ways for your glory. Amen.

KRISTINA PETERSEN

ESTHER: FOR SUCH A TIME AS THIS

BIBLE PASSAGE: THE BOOK OF ESTHER

Of all the women in the Bible, Esther has to be the one I admire the most. I find it tremendously inspiring to read how God used an ordinary woman with a sad past to bring about a great victory over evil. True, she was beautiful, but we all have different gifts: there's hope for me to do something great yet!

We may be a little envious of Esther's position as queen (who wouldn't fancy living in the lap of luxury, with fabulous clothes, the best in food and wines, beauty treatments galore and maids at our beck and call?) but if we were to walk with Esther for a few weeks, I think we would learn more than how to enjoy the glamorous life.

To start with, as an orphan, Esther's childhood can't have been easy. Despite being cared for by her cousin Mordecai, she must have known sadness, either at losing her parents or never knowing them. She was also an exile in a foreign land, never having visited the country of her fathers, but no doubt having heard many harrowing stories of the terrible siege of Jerusalem and how the Jews lost everything that was precious to them—their promised land, their king, their temple.

Yet we see in Esther not a heart torn apart by anger, bitterness or hatred, but a young woman with a gentle spirit who was loyal and obedient and found favour with everyone. Her loveliness must certainly have been more than skin deep: with a choice of hundreds of young beauties, what man would choose an arrogant, sullen or nagging wife?

I wonder whether Esther aspired to do something great, or

whether she hoped that her difficult days were over when she was chosen to be queen. My guess is the latter. Most of us prefer the quiet life, and great deeds usually require sacrifice. But it was only a little while into Esther's reign when crisis loomed.

Mordecai, the cousin who brought Esther up, refused to kneel and honour Haman, right-hand man to the king. Infuriated by this lack of respect, Haman plotted to rid himself not just of Mordecai but of the whole Jewish race. The king agreed to Haman's scheme, couched as it was in deceptive terms, not realizing that his dear queen was a Jew.

In the end, though, the tables were turned. At Mordecai's bidding, Esther pleaded with the king to spare her life and the lives of her people. This was dangerous: she had to enter the king's presence unbidden, which called for the death penalty unless pardon was offered. Fortunately, Esther found favour with the king, and he granted her request. Haman was hanged on the gallows that he had erected for Mordecai, and the Jews were allowed to defend themselves against their enemies. They killed an awesome 75,500 in one day.

Most of us may never have to risk our lives for others; the majority of our 'right place, right time' situations will probably seem 'everyday' compared to Esther's life-threatening act of obedience. Having said that, every little seed that we sow has the potential to grow into something big. Without constant effort and determination, though, these opportunities can easily slip away.

Mordecai said to Esther, 'Who knows? Perhaps you hve come to royal dignity for just such a time as this' (4:14, NRSV). Surely we have been similarly carefully placed, but are we really doing the will of God where we are, or are the 'cares and riches and pleasures of life' (Luke 8:14, NRSV)—perhaps the latest films, soaps or gossip—choking our lives, making them unproductive?

We may not be called to do something huge (not yet!), but we can be obedient in the small yet vital things—witnessing to our neighbours and colleagues, encouraging people at church, bringing up our children to honour the Lord.

Esther's obedience to Mordecai is worthy of note. Even after becoming queen, she followed his instructions as she had as a child. Obedience to parents and husbands is not so fashionable these days, even among Christians, despite both being biblical. We may even be scornful of wives who obey their husbands, while bemoaning our children's disobedience. Why do we resist obedience so much?

Perhaps we find obedience humiliating; there is something in us that strives for position and status, to be at least 'equal', preferably 'better'. But in God's kingdom, we are already equal, just different; and if we want to be great, we must humble ourselves and become the servant of all. Jesus came to serve and to obey his Father in everything, even when it meant washing his disciples' feet and suffering a criminal's death. That was not weakness, though; it was supreme strength. Service and obedience were not humiliating to Jesus, nor, it seems, to Queen Esther.

Something else I admire in Esther is her humility. Not taking God's favour for granted—as many of her ancestors had done and suffered for it—she called for a three-day fast in preparation for her unsolicited audience with the king. As Christians, we are amazingly privileged to be able to enter God's presence with confidence, but we can sometimes forget, with all our triumphant songs and claiming of promises, that the Lord still loves a sacrifice. I feel that the Lord is pleased when we kneel in respect, when we fast, when we get up early to pray, not because it is our religious duty but because we feel humbled and privileged to be in the presence of the King of kings.

One thing that I find surprising about Esther, and which, if I'm honest, makes me feel a little uncomfortable, is that she asks the king for a second day for the Jews to slaughter their enemies (9:13). Most beauty queens request world peace!

However, in the Old Testament, the things that happen can be a picture for us in our spiritual lives. Now, our struggle is no longer against flesh and blood, but against 'the rulers, against the authorities, against the powers of this dark world and against the spiritual forces of evil in the heavenly realms' (Ephesians 6:12) that would love to annihilate us. Who wouldn't like a second day to slaughter those? When these enemies are finally vanquished, there will indeed be world peace. There will be no more suffering, persecutions, fear, hatred, war, slavery, famine, illness, pain or death. Then we too will rejoice in victory over evil. For now, each one of us must 'fight the good fight of the faith' (1 Timothy 6:12).

We are all precious, vital, unique stones in God's building. That's an awesome responsibility, because stones aren't known for their ability to stretch to fill in gaps. Nobody can fit in your hole but you—not even Anne Graham-Lotz or Jackie Pullinger!

If you have a sad past, as Esther did, that's still not a barrier to being used by God. In fact, if we allow them to, our own sufferings can make us more understanding, more compassionate people. Whatever it is we are called to do, let's do it, great or small.

It's victory when we read the Bible and pray, when we walk in the Spirit, when we love and forgive others, when we reach out to the lost, care for the needy, or speak up when the authorities have got it wrong. Our enemies will try to stop us at every turn. Scared? Me too! Better dust off the armour of God, because we'll be needing it.

Reflect

- Esther courageously did what she could in her God-given position. We have all been given everything we need to fulfil the will of God for our lives. One of Esther's gifts was beauty, while ours may be more practical. Are we using our gifts courageously? Are we willing to take up our cross and follow Jesus in a life of obedience and service?
- Some of us may sigh when we look in the mirror, but inner beauty is infinitely more precious, and this we can do something about. What sort of bride would we be if we didn't make ourselves beautiful for our husband? One day Jesus will come back. Will we be ready?

✜

Prayer

Thank you, Lord, that you didn't choose me for my beauty, achieve-ments and personality; but you have made me just the way I am for a purpose. Help me to count my blessings and use the gifts and talents you have given me for your glory. Amen.
JANET EVANS

GOMER: DO YOU KNOW
HOW MUCH YOU ARE LOVED?

BIBLE PASSAGE: HOSEA 1—3

We know very little about Gomer except that she was the daughter
of Diblaim (1:3). Her story is told entirely from her husband
Hosea's viewpoint and we don't know a great deal about him
either.

Hosea was a prophet in the northern kingdom of Israel and he
lived around 760BC. He overlapped with Isaiah and Micah (both
prophets to the southern kingdom of Judah), and his time of
prophecy spans the reign of Jeroboam II and the turbulent years
after that king's death.

Hosea marries Gomer because God tells him to marry an
adulterous wife (1:2), but there are different interpretations of this.
Some believe that Hosea was told by God to marry a sinful woman,
others that God told Hosea to marry a woman who he knew would
prove unfaithful. What is clear is that their marriage is an acted-out
parable, mirroring the covenant or 'marriage' between God and
Israel. The Israelites have not kept their side of the covenant.
Surrounded by Canaanite religion, they have allowed their own
religion to be watered down with Canaanite 'gods' and the fertility
cult prevalent in that society. It didn't seem to matter very much to
them whether they worshipped God or Baal.

So, Hosea and Gomer marry and have children. Again the Lord
speaks and this time he stipulates the names of the children. The
first one is to be called Jezreel, as a reminder of the massacre

mentioned in 2 Kings 9. The second is named Lo-Ruhamah, meaning 'Not loved'. The third child is called Lo-Ammi, which means 'Not my people'. In all of this, God states clearly that he sees and knows that Israel has turned away from him. Israel may have forgotten him but he has not forgotten Israel.

It seems that Gomer is lured away by the sin around her and goes after other lovers, seeking riches and pleasure (2:5). She is looking for short-term gain in the form of food, linen, oil and drink. She doesn't see that her husband is the one who looks after her. She doesn't acknowledge him. She thinks about returning to her husband only when her lovers no longer give her what she wants. She considers going back to him not because it is the right thing to do, but because she realizes that she is better off with Hosea after all (2:7).

In the end, God tells Hosea to take Gomer back. In fact, he has to buy her back (3:2). It breaks his heart to see her chase after other lovers but now he welcomes her back, despite everything that she has done.

Gomer is not exactly a role model. She is portrayed as fickle, selfish, seeking after pleasures, not seeing or maybe not wanting to see that Hosea loves her and offers her all she can ever want—love, stability, security and much more besides. Yet we can learn from her, in the same way that Israel learnt from watching the marriage between Hosea and Gomer.

Of course we are not like her. We don't go after other lovers, like Gomer does, or after other 'gods', like Israel does. Or do we? Do we sometimes turn away from God or water down our faith with other 'gods', like money, success, status or even the more subtle ones like a prominent role in church, doing good works or being a good mother/wife/Sunday school teacher/employee? The change from worshipping the Lord to worshipping things that are good in themselves is subtle and can happen almost unnoticed. Is there anything in your life that takes on too dominant a role?

What about security? Gomer looked to other men for her security, believing that they could furnish her with the food and goods she thought she needed. Israel looked to other nations for security. What about us? Does our security lie in our bank account and mortgage? Do we have our future planned out? It's not that there is anything wrong in saving for a secure future and being good stewards, but material possessions can never give us what we really need—trust in our Father who loves us more than we can ever imagine.

Gomer did not realize that Hosea looked after her, just as Israel did not see that all good things came from God, not from the Canaanite 'gods'. The Lord of hosts supplies us with everything we need and he deserves our gratitude. It is good to acknowledge and thank the giver of all good things for what he has done for us and given to us, including those things that we might take for granted, including, of course, other people, our friends and our family, who are also gifts from him.

All this sounds rather negative. It is helpful and thought-provoking to ask ourselves where our priorities lie and whom or what we worship, but that does not mean we have to go on a guilt trip. Often, the wrong people—those who have no reason to repent at all—are the ones who take messages like Hosea's on board. If your security lies in God and he is your priority, then don't worry about how much of a Gomer you might be. You are not! Read on—the good news is still to come.

Gomer turned away from Hosea and went after other men. What did Hosea do? Israel went after other 'gods'. What did God do? It broke his heart and he tried everything he could to win Israel back. Whatever we do, God will want us back. God threatens punishment (2:9–13), not because he likes to punish but because the punishment leads to repentance and that, in turn, leads to new life.

Hosea's pleading with his wife becomes one with the voice of God addressing Israel: 'I will lead her into the desert and speak tenderly to her' (2:14). Into the desert? The desert is a hot and barren place, without water, food, shade or comfort—not the most suitable place for tender words.

Or maybe it is the most suitable place. In the desert, there are no distractions and there is no other security. In the desert, Gomer will hear her husband's words because her lovers are not there to speak to her or offer her food or drink.

We will all have our personal desert experiences at some time or other. They are part of life. Sometimes we can hear the Lord's voice more clearly in barren times. Sometimes new life can grow in the desert. I speak from personal experience: I can think of difficult times when all outward security seemed to crumble around me and I could do nothing but hang on to my Father. While I am not grateful for the pain of those times, I am grateful for what I could learn. God can use desert times to remove our imagined security and draw us closer to him.

Hosea loves Gomer despite her wayward behaviour and welcomes her back, showing his love to her again (3:1). God loves the Israelites, even though they have turned away from him. God loves us more than we can ever imagine. He loves us so much that it breaks his heart, and his is a love that will not let us go.

Gomer was not the perfect example of a woman of God, yet she was loved. We may not be like Gomer, but we also may not always be the perfect example of a Christian woman. That's OK, God loves us anyway! Nothing can separate us from his love. The Lord who sent his Son to die for us is a God of mercy and grace. You are loved.

Reflect

- Can you think of people who have turned away from God? Pray for them now and commit yourself to praying for them on a regular basis. Remember that God loves them more than we ever can, and that he longs for them to turn back to him.
- Do you sometimes feel that you don't deserve God's love? You are right, you don't; none of us does. But he loves us anyway. It's not about earning or deserving but about accepting his love. Pray that you will be able to accept his love for you.

✛

Prayer

Lord God, thank you for your immeasurable love for us. Thank you that your love is not dependent on how good we are, but on your mercy and grace alone. Thank you that we can trust in your love. Amen.
KRISTINA PETERSEN

THE GENTILE WOMAN: DOGGED FAITH

BIBLE PASSAGES: MATTHEW 15:21–28; MARK 7:24–30

Have you felt ignored or insulted recently? Such a 'slap in the face' leaves an impression on flushed cheeks. Recoiling from the blow, you're winded and unable to reply; a bruised heart sinks to the pit of your stomach as dejected eyes determine not to blink for fear of squeezing out those telltale tears.

We come to God's word expecting grace and unconditional love, but in this story we find Jesus appearing to ignore and insult a woman. Are these the kind of feelings he wanted to provoke? It's hard to believe that Jesus would be rude, so let's take another look at the story.

The woman had no right to enter the house. Jesus was attempting to keep his presence secret, possibly seeking a private retreat from the hounding crowds (Mark 7:24). This is the only record of Jesus and the disciples leaving Jewish territory, perhaps emphasizing their need to get away. Furthermore, the woman was a Gentile, trespassing over a Jewish threshold. Born a Greek, she lived in Phoenicia, situated along the Mediterranean coast of Syria (modern Lebanon). Its history haunted the Jews: God had promised all of Canaan to the Israelites, but they'd failed to expel the last of its inhabitants, and the distraction of Baal and other gods had brought bitter judgment upon them (Judges 10:6, 12).

Despite this, the woman still came, for the depth and strength of mother-love is a law unto itself. Who knows what state of cruel demonic possession her daughter was suffering? Desperation super-seded issues of etiquette and race. Nothing would hinder her approach to the famed rabbi: 'Lord, Son of David, have mercy on me! My daughter is suffering terribly from demon possession' (Matthew 15:22).

Jesus didn't answer a word, an apparent snub to her salutation and request. It's rude and insolent to ignore someone, so why this vexing silence? Was he deliberating on the Jewish–Gentile tension, or simply fed up that she'd gatecrashed his retreat? More likely, he was praying to his Father, to find out what he would have him say and do (John 6:38; 12:49).

The disciples didn't try to hide their animosity: 'Send her away,' they urged him. 'Give us a break… She's no right to be here… She's giving us a headache!' Jesus appeared to confirm their stance as he quietly remarked, 'I was sent only to the lost sheep of Israel' (Matthew 15:24).

Undeterred, she came and knelt before him, her plea for help igniting his reply: 'It is not right to take the children's bread and toss it to their dogs' (v. 26). What an insult! I can almost hear the disciples sniggering behind the woman's back. This exquisite metaphor confirmed Jesus' mission to the Jews, but the offensive terminology is breathtaking. It was customary for Jews to refer to Gentiles as 'scavenger dogs' and although Jesus used the gentler 'puppy dog', it can hardly have dulled the sting.

'Yes, Lord,' she replied, 'but even the dogs eat the crumbs that fall from their masters' table' (v. 27).

No sniggering now! Was Jesus going to perform a U-turn? 'Woman, you have great faith! Your request is granted' (v. 28).

We can't ignore this story's theological implications. Jesus had previously instructed his disciples to go out among the lost sheep of Israel and not to the Gentiles (Matthew 10:5–6). Yes, their mission would expand, but only after the resurrection (28:19). Yet here Jesus is highly commending the faith of this Gentile woman as he had done with her Roman centurion counterpart (Matthew 8:10)— above anything he'd witnessed among the Jews. Perhaps this provides a glimpse of the ready acceptance of the gospel among Gentiles, in contrast to Jewish contempt (John 1:11–13).

Theology, however, doesn't bypass our personal needs. This woman's method of approach to Jesus does much to teach and encourage us.

She knew nothing and no one else that could satisfy. It didn't do for a woman to approach a band of travelling strangers in this manner, much less Jewish men. Jesus wasn't expected in the vicinity, so surely she'd already spent time and possibly money imploring her own gods and their gurus to heal her daughter. Somehow she'd come to hear about Jesus' ministry in other regions. The testimony had aroused an expectant faith, without which she wouldn't have bothered to visit him when he suddenly turned up without prior warning. This is a reminder to acknowledge the touch of Jesus on our lives. Testimony can travel far by word of mouth, and someone's soul may well be drawn to faith as a result.

She came as one who was totally unworthy of his acceptance and blessing. Her race and religion barred her from a Jewish welcome, but, trusting in Jesus, she made her entrance. Sometimes we may also feel unworthy to approach God. Personally, I fear I test his patience sorely with my bad habits and weak will, so I succumb to doubts over whether he could truly love and accept me. But 'it is by grace you have been saved, through faith—and this not from yourselves, it is the gift of God' (Ephesians 2:8). Through Christ there is nothing that separates us from his love or prevents our approach to his throne.

Jesus countered the disciples' reservations. The disciples weren't too sure about this woman, perhaps a little embarrassed by her outburst. We may not think we're prejudiced, but it's surprising how weak the flesh can be at unexpected moments. Fallible human nature is prone to emit disapproving vibes when someone's behaviour, culture, accent, colour, work, dress, priorities, diet, faith and so on don't quite fit the prevailing social or religious code. How awful we'd feel to be perceived as a naive, prejudiced, whining, sniggering disciple!

Jesus' silence captivated her. It might have been a deterrent, but hers was a hungry faith and refused to leave without nourishment.

She couldn't even be sure that she had his attention, but he certainly had hers. In those silent moments, her focus intensified upon his face and she was drawn towards him, oblivious of the disciples, falling to her knees at his feet. That's where we need to be—infatuated with Jesus, on our knees at his feet.

She wasn't foiled by first impressions. Jesus appeared to be ignoring and insulting her, but she wasn't sidetracked into making rash judgments. Merely reading the text can hinder our comprehension, where we'd benefit from 3D glasses to get the full perspective. Written words conceal the spoken tone of voice and facial expression. If you read that I once told my daughter to mind her own business, it would be reasonable to assume that I was reprimanding her for eavesdropping on my private conversation. In reality, I'd been arranging a secret treat, so the 'reprimand' was given with an air of loving intrigue, framed by a cheeky grin, laughing eyes and a finger tapping my nose. The woman had the advantage of seeing and hearing Jesus—a smile dancing about his lips perhaps, eyes entreating her to faith, compassionate love embracing each syllable. God wants everyone to be saved and to know the truth (1 Timothy 2:3–4) so it's not in his best interests to confuse that truth with insult, then publicize it in the world's bestseller!

Our approach to scripture is more than mere reading. We're reliant on the Spirit to grant us 3D perception, enabling us to see beyond the typeset with his eyes and ears. Setting aside our immediate perceptions allows the Spirit to mould our viewpoint. Prayerful reflection takes us deeper into the living Word, enriching our lives with his insight and guidance.

'Great faith' rewarded her. Jesus commended the woman's faith-filled response, a tenacity that drew and kept her with him against all odds. Initially she hailed him with a polite and appropriate greeting. Through silence, then subsequent dialogue, however, she engaged with the Son of God, who drew her towards him, inciting her to faith. She accepted her Gentile position, but had faith to reach out for the future promise he'd unveiled—she'd be ready and

waiting second in line! Her expectant, steadfast resolve proved fertile soil for his timely seeds, the resultant fruit a forerunner of its time.

The development of our relationship with Jesus depends on our readiness to stay by his side. He draws us, even woos us into deeper faith, but when the going gets tough it's tempting to run away or seek solace through other means. Here our friend inspires us to look beyond the immediate difficulties, to draw up close and kneel at his feet, even when he chooses not to give an immediate answer.

If Jesus granted our wish list at a moment's notice, our faith would be stunted and our relationship little more than cupboard love. Are we willing to trust him in silence, in discipline, in our confusion or misunderstanding? The Gentile woman had nothing to give, but faith was focused through silence, strengthened through trust, and encouraged through dialogue. She learnt to lean on God for his answer, in his time—and so can we.

Reflect

- Are we sometimes surprised, even shocked, by Jesus' behaviour? Have we tried to squeeze him into the mould of society's acceptable conduct? Jesus only said and did what his Father told him. (See Matthew 21:12–13; John 6:38; 12:49.)
- Do we approach Jesus in prayer as a formality, a religious duty, with a long list of requests, or from a burning desire to spend time with him, to draw close to him and to learn from him? (See Luke 10:38–42; 18:10–14.)
- How great is your faith? How big is a mustard seed? (See Luke 7:1–10; Matthew 17:20.)
- The gilt-edged promise of salvation runs throughout scripture. Do we get bogged down with a few verses, our own life, a difficult situation? Ask God to broaden your thinking to his bigger picture of salvation, and what part he wants you to play. (See Genesis 22:18; Isaiah 56:7; Matthew 28:19; John 1:10–13; Ephesians 2:14–19; Revelation 15:4)

✤

Prayer

Lord, in the words of the father of the deaf and dumb boy whom you healed, I do believe; help me in my unbelief. I know where I need to be, but disillusionment and temporary quick-fix solutions can distract me from coming to you—my only source of true peace, guidance and fulfilment. Here I am, Lord. Please renew my first love and passion for Jesus. Amen.

ANNE LE TISSIER

ELIZABETH: ONE OF THE DEEP PEOPLE

BIBLE PASSAGE: LUKE 1

The village was buzzing! They couldn't remember a day like it. There had been embarrassment in the past—a sense of not knowing where to put themselves when Elizabeth had stood watching their children playing in front of her house. They had seen the anguish in her face, which she'd tried to hide behind a smile that didn't reach her eyes.

In a society where a man's blessedness is reckoned by a head count of his children, how does a barren woman cope? Where does she find her self-esteem? How does she go on believing in the goodness of God? There is a sense of isolation, of being different. She doesn't want to be different and she doesn't want pity either. She wants to be normal—to be a mother.

Thankfully, the scriptures that Elizabeth had known since childhood did not pretend that 'everything in the garden was lovely' for those who believe. The scriptures set down the people's struggles and desert wanderings, as well as the triumphs and feeding by still waters. Elizabeth could put herself alongside other women who had believed and yet had seen suffering and tragedy invade their faithful lives. She was one with them.

She knew that her people's God was one who offered the shadow of his wings (Psalm 17:8) and had compassion on those in trouble and sorrow of every kind (Psalm 116:3-6). In fact, he expected them to be honest about their feelings and to turn to him in times of need.

The church today is sometimes guilty of triumphalism, leaving those who have insoluble problems, and suffer anguish because of it, feeling guilty. Their testimony of God's faithfulness to them and his presence with them in the deepest pit of their experience is not good enough. The testimonies most lauded are those that tell of the miraculous resolution of problems, the healings, the provision of large amounts of cash. Yet if we get close to those who suffer and who are honest about it, we find marks of grace that do not develop in those for whom everything always goes well—or those who find a theological way of convincing themselves that it does so.

Elizabeth knew all of this and, along with her husband Zechariah, she lived an upright life, obedient to God's commandments. They continued to observe the obligations of the Law despite the fact that God had not spoken to Israel by any prophet for 400 years and had not given them personally their hearts' desire.

Now the longed-for child had been born. The days had long gone when the couple had hoped for one by natural means. Yes, they knew about Abraham and Sarah, Jacob and Rachel, and Elkanah and Hannah. Perhaps they had given a passing thought to the possibility that they would have a miracle too. With the promised birth of a Messiah, perhaps Elizabeth, along with many other Jewish women, had a little thought cherished at the back of her consciousness that she would be his mother. But these were only passing thoughts. It was no use building any hopes on them. Now dreams had become reality. The miracle had taken place, its imminence announced by an angel to Zechariah when he was on priestly duty in the temple (Luke 1:8–25).

God had chosen Zechariah and Elizabeth to be the parents of a special child. Although Zechariah was struck dumb because he had not immediately believed the angel's words, he would have found a way to convey the angel's message to his wife. What she learned was more than enough satisfaction for the years of lonely waiting.

As a believing woman, she would have been thrilled to the core to hear that her child would be the one to bring God's people back to him. Not everyone had waited faithfully for the fulfilment of his promises as she and Zechariah had, and repentance was needed to get them back on track. Her heart must have raced to know that the spirit and power in her son would be those of Elijah, one of Israel's greatest prophets. Reconciliation and repentance would be the results of his preaching, and the objective would be to prepare God's people for the Messiah's coming.

What a challenge this is for today's Christian parents! What fears and hopes are held for their children's future? Is the greatest fear that they will end up with a massive debt from their student loan, or that they will never afford to get on to the property ladder? These fears are understandable in responsible parents, but does anyone hope that their children will end up as poorly paid missionaries or pastors, or workers with the homeless?

I remember vividly an incident that occurred when I was a young Christian. A godly (and wealthy) couple, to whom I looked up with great admiration, expressed dismay when their daughter developed a romantic attachment to a Christian student worker who was considering a call to become a clergyman. 'He'll never have any money!' was their worried reaction. I came from a less well-heeled background anyway, but I simply didn't understand and went home very sad.

Is there today a deep desire that Christian offspring will follow God whatever the cost in terms of material benefit, physical safety and social status? That is certainly where Zechariah and Elizabeth stood.

So the child was born and named John, much to the surprise of the whole village. Before that, however, a greater miracle had taken place. Elizabeth's kinswoman, Mary, had conceived a child although she was still a virgin. She was the one for whom the greatest dream had come true: she would be the mother of Israel's Messiah.

In Mary's visit to Elizabeth we see one of the most tender scenes in the Bible (Luke1:39–41). Many artists have depicted the scene and tried to capture the amazing moment when Mary entered Elizabeth's house. These kinswomen knew what was important in life. Their hopes and expectations for the redemption of God's people were foremost in their thinking, dreams and ambitions. They were overwhelmed with a sense of privilege at the central role they would play in its coming. Their sense of fellowship and shared joy are a delightful example of how godly women can encourage each other in faith. They can weep and rejoice together; they can pray and dream together; and they can wonder together at the ways of God.

Friends of many years, cousins and aunts and nieces, as well as mothers and daughters, can form a supportive network that is always there for the times when only those who have known us best and longest can fully share both the hurting places and the deepest joys life brings.

Open to God's word through the Spirit, Elizabeth immediately recognized Israel's Messiah in the child Mary was bearing. Her baby did so as well, as he leapt in her womb. The Spirit was convincing them all of what was afoot. In the loud voice often associated with prophecy in the Bible, Elizabeth spoke words from God (Luke 1:42–45). They are words of certainty, encouragement and humility.

While inspired by God's Spirit, the words nevertheless reflect Elizabeth's character and depth of understanding of God's ways through knowledge of the scriptures and obedience to them. The Spirit takes what we know, the things we believe from his word, along with the faith and experience we have, and brings them together in us to form words that glorify him and point to his purposes. This is the spirit of prophecy so beautifully demonstrated in Elizabeth and, of course, in Mary and Zechariah soon afterwards.

If we want to be filled with the Spirit and be used to bring his word for today to his people, we need to soak ourselves in the scriptures and try to understand its application to all the circumstances of our life's experience, hanging on in faith where we do not understand. Then we shall be deep people, and deep things will emerge from our lives in words and actions inspired by God's Spirit.

Elizabeth's unquestioning acceptance of Mary's claim to

continued virginity and her prophetic understanding of what was happening must have been very important to Mary. Perhaps because of the miracle taking place within herself, Elizabeth found it easier to accept than it would have been only months previously. But there was such a depth of trust between the two women that it did not seem to occur to her to hold on to even a tiny doubt. Perhaps it was the strength of the Spirit within her that made doubt impossible. Whichever it was, Mary found the support she so much needed at this time.

If all her family had even initially shown the misunderstanding that Joseph showed, Mary would have had a much harder time of it. In addition, if there was any residual doubt in herself about what she had seen and heard, it would have been dispelled by Elizabeth's greeting, which complemented that of the angel Gabriel. Elizabeth declared that Mary was blessed among women both for the child she was bearing and for her willing acceptance of God's plan.

Godly Elizabeth! She is an example to all women who want to glorify God. We must stick at it when our faith is tested. When life goes well in the accepted way for other women and we seem to be left out, we must hold on in trust. We must be led by God's Spirit and never let anything or anyone make us feel inferior because we do not have the things that other women take for granted.

We can then encourage others with the comfort we receive from God and from other women. We can know that he has a purpose for our lives just as much as for theirs. We can be a part of the network of women who encourage and strengthen each other in an unbelieving and sceptical world. We can demonstrate that it is possible to live lives of faith in all circumstances, and we can encourage others in doing so.

Reflect

- Which women are important to you as those who encourage you in faith and with whom you could share your deepest sadness

and greatest joys? Thank God for them and, when appropriate, let them know how much they matter to you. Perhaps write a note of thanks to them.
- Are there women to whom you are important in this way? Perhaps you hesitate to think so. If there are not, ask God to show you whom you could encourage, sharing his life in you with them.
- Do you do all you can to maintain supportive networks of godly women?

✢

Prayer

Lord Jesus, King of glory, yet despised, rejected, spat upon, at times we only feel the pain.

Help us to hear, when our heads are bowed with grief, the swish of your garment and to look up and see the kindness in your eyes.

Thank you for those who are to us your touch, your eyes, your love, who bring you near to where we stoop.

Through our pains make us strong, as we know your love in ways we could not before and to go on to share that love with others in their pain.

ANNE ROBERTS

THE WOMAN WITH AN ISSUE OF
BLOOD: HEALED AND SET FREE

BIBLE PASSAGES: LUKE 8:43–48; MARK 5:24–34

Perhaps she'd been a woman of society. It would never do to be seen with the rabble crowding around Jesus. Neither could she call out across an open space as did the ten men with leprosy, whom Jesus encountered on his way to Jerusalem (Luke 17:11–19). Perhaps, in any case, she feared rejection. With a condition like hers there were always those willing to press home the idea that uncleanness was attached to unworthiness and getting what you deserved. 'Who sinned, this man or his parents?' the disciples asked about the man born blind (John 9:2).

When people say it, you begin to believe it. You even had to declare it yourself! 'Unclean! Unclean!' 'Sticks and stones may break my bones but names will never hurt me!' we used to retaliate as children. Oh, but they do! In addition, simply being among this crowd without declaring herself was asking for trouble. Approaching a rabbi, a man known to be a law keeper, in her condition, was social suicide.

She must have had money at one time, perhaps while her husband still acknowledged her as his wife. In those days she'd paid many doctors for so-called cures and none of them had worked. One suggestion was to 'set her in a place where two ways meet and let her hold a cup of wine in her right hand, and let someone come behind and frighten her and say, "Arise from thy flux."' Elsewhere it was recommended that the woman carry about with her a barley corn taken from the droppings of a white donkey.

For twelve years she had been bleeding and seeking a cure, and had only got worse. She was of no use to her husband. He couldn't come near her to enjoy the legitimate pleasures of married life. It follows that she couldn't bear him any children. If she already had children, she couldn't look after them or supervise her husband's household or entertain his guests. She was useless and hopeless.

Then she began to hear about a man who could heal sick people. He didn't seem to withhold his powers from those believed unclean like her. He had time for other outcasts like tax collectors. So, surely, he would be kind to her. Or would he? After so many years of dashed hopes, broken dreams, loneliness and despair, did she dare to try again? She must have spent sleepless nights coming to her decision and wondering how she would put it into action.

Rumour had it that he was one of those holy men whose power flowed out through the hem of his cloak. Perhaps that would work. She would cover herself completely, as many women did for various reasons. No one would recognize her. She would choose a time when the crowd was pressing around him (that wouldn't be difficult), get next to him, drop something; stoop to pick it up and touch the hem of his cloak.

It may not seem very daring to us, but to her it was heart-stopping. What if he noticed? He would surely condemn her publicly. The crowd would turn on her and scream at her for her audacity and for contaminating them. They might even stone her and hound her out of town. The shame would be as excruci-ating as anything she had suffered in the last twelve years.

This woman is not easily put off, however. She has not accepted that she is worthless. She wants her life back. She has not given up on herself, or life, or God. The risk is worth taking. So she carries out her plan—and it works. She knows immediately that she is healed. The heaviness, the nausea, the constant flow have all gone!

'She was freed from her suffering' (Mark 5:29). It had held her in chains for twelve years, and now she is free. For just a second she is in her own private heaven. Then, back to earth with a bump!

'Who touched me?' (Luke 8:45). How could he know? Jesus speaks with authority and he waits, so, more fearful than at any time in her life before, she throws herself on the ground at his feet and tells him the whole story.

Jesus often asked a person to give more than they had come willing to give. Some refused and went away empty. This woman gave all he asked and went away full. He was able to give her far more than just physical healing because she was willing, despite her fear.

First, he could tell her that she wasn't healed by a magic trick, but by her faith. Some would have brought her faith into question as she had pleaded with God for mercy over so many years and apparently gone unheard. Jesus looked into her eyes and told her that he knew she was a woman of faith. He made sure she knew that he was not just a purveyor of power, but a man of compassion. There was no condemnation in his eyes, just recognition of the hard road she had had to walk, and all the love and affirmation for which she longed.

For a moment the crowd may as well not have been there. She went away with far more than she had dreamed. She went away with *shalom*, the word translated as 'peace' but meaning far more than absence of worry. It means wholeness of body, mind and spirit. The translation could read, 'Go into wholeness' (Mark 5:34; Luke 8:48).

Jesus' public announcement of her healing would also mean that she would not be turned away by the priest when she went along with her thank offering for official recognition of her new situation. In addition to the physical suffering, she was freed from the loneliness and isolation, from lack of self-worth. She was free to move again in the mainstream of her religion and of her faith community.

All of that, Jesus knew, and she could see in his eyes that he felt her joy. She knew instinctively that there was more to this man than she had realized. Who was he? She must have lain awake that night remembering. 'Daughter.' Did he really say, 'Daughter'?

Uncleanness in the biblical sense is something with which we may not be familiar. The Quechua Indians of South America knew all about it. When groups of them heard a dramatized tape in the

Quechua language of the story of the woman with the issue of blood, in every case they sobbed with joy. They knew what it was to be 'unclean' in the eyes of neighbouring tribes. To hear that God did not regard them in that way, but associated himself with those on whom others looked down, was better news than they could have hoped for.

It isn't only that kind of treatment that makes people feel unable to hold up their heads in public, however. What we know, or think, people think of us is enormously important to our self-esteem. We can be destroyed by it. We can be kept from receiving our healing because of it, if we even suspect that what they think is somehow a reflection of what God thinks.

There are thousands outside the Church who believe they are not good enough for God because, rightly or wrongly, they see the Church as keener to face them with the fact that they have sinned than with the fact that they are precious to God and that he longs to show them forgiveness and compassion.

We may have had faith, but if we do something that the faith community judges unacceptable, even our genuine repentance (if such is necessary) may not be good enough for them. They have their standards and they hold those standards over our heads. They will protest that we are welcome, but their words lack warmth and we know we can never be counted as one of the community again. They remain uninterested in our pleas that we should be heard and our integrity respected. We remain outcast.

Who will be the hem of Jesus' garment to such folk? That, surely, is what Christians must be. We must be the point of contact, the means of entry. Preaching, teaching, visiting, evangelism, caring must all be hems of his garment. The unacceptable, the failures, the ostracized, must hear that they can come near and touch him, that he longs to listen and to touch them with his healing and forgiving love. But first we must know it for ourselves. We must acknowledge our own uncleanness through sin, experience the deep forgiving love of Jesus for us, and know our great worth to him. From this position and in this love we can live the message.

Not all healing from the kind of abuse suffered by this woman results in immediate wholeness. Those who have been made to feel worthless do not always react kindly to being told otherwise. They may feel patronized. They may be very angry inside, and when this anger spills over, they make themselves even more unacceptable, but they may not be able to avoid it. Emotional hurts inflict very deep wounds. Unless we understand their anger, their sense of being lost and their desperation, we will not be the hem of Jesus' garment to them. We shall pull up our skirts for fear of contamination and leave them worse than they were before, having confirmed to them their lack of self-worth.

There is no kinder ministry than bringing the hem of Jesus' garment to those who are hurting through abuse and mis-understanding. Those who have done it for us have done what lightly made promises of prayer and protestations of love without action could never do. They bring us Jesus.

Reflect

- Have you had an experience that made you feel unclean and unworthy? Have you been able to bring it to Jesus? Have you accepted the experience as part of what Jesus can use to help you understand others who suffer rejection?
- Have you ever grown impatient with yourself or with someone else who did not recover quickly from an experience of rejection? Have you learnt patience and compassion in such matters?
- Is there some action you need to take in order to bring the hem of Jesus' garment to someone who is suffering rejection? Pray for great sensitivity as you do so.
- Pray for yourself if you feel unclean because of the attitude others have taken towards you, and seek help from someone who you know will bring Jesus to you.

✣

Prayer

Lord Jesus, King of glory, yet despised, rejected, spat upon,
at times we only feel the pain.
When our heads are bowed with grief,
help us to hear the swish of your garment
and to look up and see the kindness in your eyes.
Thank you for those who are to us your touch, your eyes, your love,
who bring you near to where we stoop.
Through our pains make us strong,
as we know your love in ways we could not before,
and help us to go on to share that love with others in their pain.
ANNE ROBERTS

THE POOR WIDOW:
GIVING EVERYTHING

BIBLE PASSAGES: MARK 12:41–44; LUKE 21:1–4

Imagine the scene. A shabbily dressed woman rests her flushed cheek against a cool marble pillar as she basks in the luxurious shade of Solomon's Colonnade. The Outer Court is heaving—a mass of pilgrims bringing temple tributes and freewill offerings prior to the great Passover feast. How she relishes her opportunities to visit the temple, for it is the one place where her wretched loneliness dissolves in the shadow of Yahweh's close proximity.

She has heard rumours of a man who caused mayhem in this court the previous day: overturning the tables of money changers, scattering coinage and livestock in all directions, he'd angrily condemned the state of God's house of prayer. Sadly, however, the bullies and bullocks are back with a vengeance!

Taking a deep breath, she plunges into the milling throng. Heading towards the eastern wall, she recalls the psalms of ascent being sung on her recent journey: 'I call on the Lord in my distress, and he answers me... My help comes from the Lord, the Maker of heaven and earth... The Lord will keep me from all harm—he will watch over my life' (Psalm 120:1; 121:2, 7). With a sigh of relief, she reaches the Beautiful Gate and enters the Court of the Women, blissfully distanced from all those bleating sheep.

A smile tickles her dry, cracked lips as she glimpses her goal beneath the gallery: 13 gleaming trumpet-shaped funnels, each allotted for specific treasury contributions. Her sense of purpose revived, she presses on towards the opposite wall, passing as she does so a tired-looking man sitting with his head in his hands, subtly observing her bare, dirty feet as they shuffle by. He looks up and, fixing an enlightened gaze upon her back, watches her weaving through the crowd.

A Levite brushes past, his cool, linen tunic seeming to mock the discomfort of her coarse, dark sackcloth. Choosing her 'trumpet', she stands in stark contrast to the wealthy contributors sporting colourful tassels on the hems of their long flowing robes with large, leather money pouches hanging from their belts. No tinkling ornaments for the widow; no rings about her ankles or silver threaded headband; no crescent pendant around her neck or bangles on her wrists.

Discreetly placing a hand beneath her cloak, she finds the cloth girdle about her waist within whose secret pocket is her entire livelihood. Without hesitation she grasps the two lepta and drops them into the treasury. As the psalm says, 'a defender of widows is God in his holy dwelling' (Psalm 68:5).

Gratitude and adoration shine from her worn, bronzed face as she melts anonymously into the crowd—anonymous, that is, to thousands of pilgrims, but acknowledged and esteemed throughout history by the one so touched by her devotion: 'I tell you the truth, this poor widow has put more into the treasury than all the others. They all gave out of their wealth; but she, out of her poverty, put in everything—all she had to live on' (Mark 12:43–44).

The widow was just one of many women whose heart ached in mourning and whose body ached in poverty, but something about her so stirred the heart of God that he prompted his Son as she walked by. Without a word being passed between them, Jesus recognized her widowhood, for she would have worn the customary sackcloth (a dark coarse mesh of goats' hair) used by those in mourning (Genesis 38:14, 19; 37:34; Joel 1:8).

Widows were, by nature of their circumstances, poor. Jesus' description of her as a 'poor widow' (Mark 12:43) merely accentu-ated the height of her poverty, quite possibly evidenced by a lack of sandals on her feet or flesh on her undernourished frame. Widows were vulnerable to extortion and had limited means of earning money, so he required no further proof concerning her lack of material wealth or possessions.

Jesus knows all about our circumstances, too. He never expects more than what we are able to give, but neither does he excuse any shortfall.

What did the widow give? 'Two very small copper coins, worth only a fraction of a penny' (Mark 12:42). These two lepta, or 'mites', were the smallest coins in circulation at the time. Their value in today's monetary terms is not even half a penny. Perhaps we do not feel that we have very much to give, but we probably have more than the widow's 1/40th of a penny.

'She… put in everything—all she had to live on' (v. 44). Is there a tendency to think subconsciously that the widow had something, no matter how little, to return home to? A jar on the mantelpiece, a few notes underneath the mattress, perhaps? Dare we even begin to entertain the thought that she gave everything?

'All' is such an easy word to skim over until we put our own names in the scenario. The entire balance of various current and savings accounts, the value of our car and possessions, the income from our spouse or anyone who would bail us out if necessary—the whole lot, without compromise. No hidden life insurance, pension, health care scheme, premium bonds, inheritance or wealthy benefactor. Not even a well-stocked freezer or larder—'all' she had to live on.

How did she give it? 'They… out of their wealth; but she, out of her poverty' (v. 44). Despite their sizeable gifts, the rich were so wealthy that their offerings barely made a dent in their 'millions' back at home. The widow, however, had barely anything to give, but she sacrificially offered the entire amount. As this scene unfolded, Jesus was on the brink of giving all he could for the human race and, in so doing, making the ultimate sacrifice. No wonder his heart was moved as he watched her giving all that she could, holding nothing back for herself.

When we give of money, time, talents or resources, just how

much of a sacrifice is it to us? Does it even touch our personal security, pleasures and comforts?

She gave willingly and joyfully. The text does not mention this, but the widow would not come so highly commended if she had given in any other way. 'God loves a cheerful giver', not one who comes reluctantly or under compulsion of their leaders (2 Corinthians 9:7).

She gave discreetly. Jesus had just castigated the expensively dressed teachers of the law whose wealth, in part, was gained from the extortion of widows. Similarly, he objected to hypocrites whose giving was accompanied by great show and ceremony to boost their reputation and self-esteem. Jesus so admired this woman that we can surely assume that she gave discreetly and privately—honouring and revering the one who saw what she did in secret (Matthew 6:4).

She gave generously. Even with her meagre offering, she could quite reasonably have kept a coin for herself, but such was her generosity that she gave to God an offering that continues to remind us of the generous gift Christ gave for us: 'Freely you have received, freely give' (Matthew 10:8).

Why did the widow give her gift? First, she loved God. 'God so loved the world that he gave his one and only Son' (John 3:16), and she so loved God that she gave everything back to him. The widow was, no doubt, a faithful Israelite who respected her obligation to support the temple ministry, but it would be hard to believe that one so poor and so alone gave her entire livelihood for the sake of religion, tradition or expectation. She gave freely, willingly and un-reservedly out of love for her heavenly Father, divine protector and sovereign friend.

Second, she trusted God. 'Perfect love drives out all fear' (1 John 4:18). She had no fear for her future, or even where her next meal would come from, because she knew that the one who loved her would care for her needs. Her trust in God's faithfulness provided all the security she would ever need. Jesus would not have seen a pained expression as she let go of her very last penny, but one of peace and contentment, the fruit of her steadfast faith in God.

Similarly, the extent to which we are willing to give is determined by the extent to which we trust God to meet our needs. Are we therefore being asked to give up our income, sell our homes and possessions, liquidate our bank accounts and live on the streets in order to give our all to the church? Probably not! In fact, God loves to give good gifts to his children (Matthew 7:11; James 1:17). This story does pose some challenges, however. In whom or what have we placed our security? Who decides how to use our possessions, time and talents? Does a desire for extras, luxuries or a nest egg overshadow our trust in God to provide what he knows we actually need, and so limit our giving?

Reflect

- What do we give back to God's work and ministry of our finances, possessions, time and talent?
- How do we give it—sacrificially or painlessly, joyfully or resentfully, discreetly or pompously, generously or meagrely?
- Why do we give it—out of love or obligation, desire or tradition, from security or to earn favour?
- Ponder these words: 'But just as you excel in everything—in faith, in speech, in knowledge, in complete earnestness and in your love for us—see that you also excel in this grace of giving' (2 Corinthians 8:7).

❖

Prayer

Lord, help me to keep my life free from the love of money and self-interest, so that I might always respond to the prompting of your Spirit and joyfully share in all that you have entrusted to my care. Amen.
ANNE LE TISSIER

SAPPHIRA: STRUCK DOWN
BECAUSE OF LIES

BIBLE PASSAGE: ACTS 5:1–11

Sapphira is a biblical name meaning 'beautiful gem' but, understandably, even today there aren't many girls of that name in the church. Sapphira probably wasn't a popular choice of name for newborn babes in the early church either; who would want to name their daughter after someone who died for lying to God?

Her story comes in Acts 5. It was early days in the Church, not too long after Pentecost. Several thousand believers were meeting together in the temple and their number was growing as the word of God spread with great power. The apostles were performing many signs and wonders and all the believers were one in heart and mind, eating together and sharing their worldly goods. Some were even selling fields and possessions, bringing the proceeds to the apostles for those in need. What a church!

Enter husband and wife Ananias and Sapphira, who sold a piece of property that belonged to them. Sadly, they decided to lie about the price and donate only part of the money. It was Ananias who took the gift to the apostles. 'How is it that Satan has so filled your heart that you have lied to the Holy Spirit?' Peter asked Ananias, acting on a word of knowledge. 'Didn't [the land] belong to you… And… wasn't the money at your disposal? You have not lied to men but to God' (vv. 3–4). Immediately, Ananias fell down and died. Imagine that happening in your church when the offering is taken up!

Three hours later, Sapphira arrived on the scene, unaware of her husband's death. 'Is this the price you and Ananias got for the land?' asked Peter. 'Yes, that is the price,' she agreed (v. 8). And Sapphira fell down dead too. Unsurprisingly, great fear came upon the whole church following this tragic episode.

This is a sobering story, which we may have trouble reconciling with the God we think we know and love, perhaps because we recognize ourselves here and balk at the severity of the punishment. One lie—surely that doesn't deserve death? We perhaps forget that every lie has its origins in the father of lies, the devil, and that God had had enough of half-hearted sacrifices and 'religion for show' in the Old Testament. Think of Jesus' beautiful new Church, about to be defiled! Read Malachi, if you dare; it's scary stuff.

But what of Sapphira? What a terrible mistake she made. Why didn't she refuse to lie? Not only would she have lived, but perhaps Ananias would have come to his senses too. We can only speculate, but maybe Ananias was very persuasive; we all know people like that. Or perhaps he made all the decisions in their marriage. Of course, it's possible that Ananias and Sapphira enjoyed plotting together, or maybe she was the scheming one, sending Ananias to the apostles to do her dirty work. Which scenario would it have been if it had been you?

Let's take a closer look. First, let's think about persuasion. This is such a big issue; words have such power. How many of us can be persuaded to go along with somebody else when we know it's not right—not just partners, but parents, bosses, children (experts in the art of persuasion!) and even friends? The enemy is not picky about whom he will use to tempt us. Jesus once said, 'Get behind me, Satan' to his dear friend Peter (Matthew 16:23), who honestly thought that he was being helpful.

Is there someone in your life who nags, cajoles, threatens or simply suggests that you should do something wrong? Then, out of fear, not wanting to offend or just to keep the peace, you give in, feeling guilty because you know that what you are doing or allowing is wrong. I can't help thinking of Maxine Carr, who lied to protect her boyfriend, Ian Huntley, the murderer of the Soham schoolgirls. Her life will never be the same again.

It takes courage to stand up for what is right, and to keep standing, but if ever there was a time for us women to be assertive, this is it. Better to stand up to an angry husband, father or boss than to fall into sin and face God. Consider what happened to Sapphira! I don't say this lightly; some of us struggle with difficult relationships. But we must obey God, for if he is our Saviour, he is also our Lord. Pray for the person who's being difficult, love them, forgive them, walk away from them if you have to, but don't let them persuade you to sin.

God has promised, in 1 Corinthians 10:13, that he will never allow us to be tempted beyond what we can bear (not even by the relentless teenager!). Shadrach, Meshach and Abednego are great examples of steadfastness in the face of persuasion: they refused to worship King Nebuchadnezzar's statue, even though the punishment was death. 'The God we serve is able to save us,' they told the king boldly. 'But even if he does not... we will not... worship the image of gold you have set up.' Read Daniel 3 if you don't know the end of that story: it's tremendously encouraging.

It's possible that Sapphira didn't need persuasion, however. She may, through naivety or apathy, have simply followed Ananias' instructions. Consider the following narratives. Ananias: 'OK to say we sold the field for this amount?' Sapphira: 'Whatever!' or 'Anything you say, darling!'

This is grossly oversimplified, of course, but Sapphira may have been happy for Ananias to make decisions in their marriage—relying on him too much, perhaps. We must beware of allowing our spiritual lives to be propped up by anybody else; what if the prop were removed? Would we bother going to church if nobody else in our family did, if our friends stopped going, or if the minister left?

We are so familiar with the idea of obeying parents and husbands and respecting those in authority that we could almost forget that our men are only human (sorry, guys!). We must remember that Jesus says that only those who love him more than parents, children and even their own lives are worthy to be his disciples (Luke 14:26). We need our own living relationship with God, loving and obeying him above all others.

We can't afford to be half-hearted. Jesus told the Laodicean church that because they were lukewarm, he would spit them out of his mouth (Revelation 3:16)—a fate definitely to be avoided! Misplaced trust can also be fatal; it is so easy to get caught up with a charming person, but just because they are charismatic it doesn't mean that they are godly. Jesus warned us to beware of false leaders who look like cute, woolly sheep but who are wolves, leading us to sin (Matthew 7:15). In the book of Acts (17:11), the Bereans studied the word of God to see if what the apostle Paul said was true. That's the way to be!

Sapphira should have done that, but perhaps it was she, and not Ananias, who was the brains behind the evil scheme, wanting to look generous but keep her worldly lifestyle. The enemy loves anything like this, especially if it involves other people with deception, gossip, lies and complaining in the church. Anything he can think of to destroy the church, he will encourage, all the way to our deaths, and the more people we take with us, the better.

Does this make you sit up? It does me! Thank God that, because of Jesus' sacrifice on the cross, there is forgiveness if we confess our sin and repent. Sapphira could have done that. Even at the last minute, she could have said to Peter, 'Actually, no, that wasn't the price…' She chose not to, but we can choose differently.

We may have to shake off the habit of a lifetime of pleasing or controlling other people. It takes courage as well as conviction to stand up and say both to ourselves and to others, 'I'm not doing that!' But God will bless us for our obedience, so much more than we can imagine.

Let's go back to names. I wonder what your friends would give you as a middle name. Laughter? Mercy? Or might they name you after somebody great and inspiring? One day we will be given a new name, by Jesus himself. I'd be happy with Faith, or Mary, after the woman who sat at Jesus' feet, but I wouldn't want Sapphira as my middle name. Would you?

Reflect

- Do we allow others to dictate how we live our lives, or are we led by God?
- Do we lean too much on others for our own spiritual life?

⁘

Prayer

Lord, help me to stand up for what is right. Please forgive me for the times I have allowed myself to be led into sin, or have led others astray. Thank you for the people you have put in my life. Help me not to rely on them, but to be an example to them of godliness, and to rely on you. Amen.

JANET EVANS

RHODA: OUR GOD OF SURPRISES

BIBLE PASSAGE: ACTS 12:1–19

The year is between AD41 and 44. It is night-time. The believers are gathered together in a large house somewhere in Jerusalem, praying. They are frightened. One of their number has already been executed and now another, Peter, has been arrested and is about to be killed. They are frightened, but they have not given up their faith in God's ability to work a miracle. They are praying for Peter's release.

Suddenly, there is a knock on the door. Who could that be at this time of night? An interloper or a spy? A friend? Rhoda is sent to the door to answer. She is only a servant girl, but she has the responsible task of distinguishing between friend and foe at the door in these dangerous times. She asks who it is and recognizes Peter's voice. She is so excited that she runs to tell the others. But they don't believe her. Peter is in a heavily guarded prison; he can't possibly be at the door! Besides, Rhoda is only a servant and a woman, so who would believe her anyway? 'You're out of your mind,' they tell her. When she keeps insisting that it is Peter, they say, 'It must be his angel' (Acts 12:15).

In the meantime, Peter keeps knocking at the door, worried about waking the neighbours. Finally, they let him in. Finally, they believe Rhoda. Peter quietens them down, knowing that he and they are all in danger if they are found, and explains what has happened.

Rhoda's part

Rhoda may not be top of our list of Bible women to take as a role model, yet she plays a small but significant part in a story that is not only about the growth of the early Church, but also about the way God acted then and acts now.

The Church was growing and had started to include Gentile believers. Paul had had his Damascus Road experience and had been converted (Acts 9), but had not yet started his extensive missionary journeys to the Gentiles.

Peter, the same Peter who had been called 'the Rock' by Jesus (Matthew 16:18), the same Peter who had denied Jesus three times (John 18:15–18, 25–27) and had been reinstated so painfully that morning on the beach after the resurrection (John 21:15–19), was one of the leaders of the Church.

The believers had just started to be called 'Christians' (Acts 11:26), but they were not popular. King Herod (Herod Agrippa I, grandson of Herod the Great and nephew of Herod Antipas, whom we know from the Gospels) was persecuting the Christians, partly to win the favour of the Jews (Acts 12:1–3). In fact, James had already been executed. They had arrested Peter, but they didn't want to execute him during the feast of Unleavened Bread (just as Jesus could not be executed during the Passover), so they put him in prison to kill him after the feast.

They made sure that Peter couldn't escape: bound with chains, with four soldiers guarding him, he had no chance of fleeing. He didn't seem too worried. He just went to sleep, and the angel who came to free him had to wake him up. Peter got up, the chains fell off him and he followed the angel through doors that opened miraculously. He thought he was dreaming and only realized that his escape was really happening when the angel disappeared and left him in the middle of Jerusalem.

Peter realized that he was in danger and immediately went to find his friends. They were meeting in Mary's house. She was the mother of John Mark (presumed to be the same Mark who wrote the Gospel). A believer herself, she had the courage to open her large house to other believers. The house had an outer entrance, separating the main room from the road. Rhoda, the servant, had to guard this entrance, making sure no unwanted guests entered.

In it together

Peter knew where to find his friends because they were all in one place. No keeping worries to themselves for them; they were all in it together. Peter was one of their number. They could not employ a lawyer to get him out of prison and they could not write a petition. They did the only thing they could do, the most effective action of all: they prayed. Not just for five minutes but for hours, even days, for as long as Peter was imprisoned.

What do you do when you have a problem? What does your church do? Do we share our worries and our joys or do we keep them private? Do we have a close group of believing friends who will stand with us in prayer? In our society, we often keep our fears and sorrows hidden behind our closed front door. Maybe we can take these first believers as an example.

Unexpected answer!

The Christians prayed for Peter's release. They prayed fervently, but didn't seem really to believe that God would answer their prayers. Maybe they had also prayed for the release of James and had been disappointed. James had been executed (Acts 12:2). Why God chose to release Peter and not James is not a question we can answer. I believe that death is not necessarily a catastrophe for the person dying, as they go on to the next stage of their life, but it can be a disaster for those who stay behind. God had one plan for James and another for Peter. Only God knows why that is so. So

Peter's friends prayed for his release, knowing that only a miracle could free him.

When Rhoda answers the knock on the door, she recognizes not only Peter's voice but more than that: she recognizes that their prayer has been answered, that God has chosen to reveal his power by releasing Peter from a heavily guarded prison. She believes. In fact, she is so excited that she forgets to open the door and runs to tell the others.

They don't believe her. They have prayed but are not expecting such an immediate answer. Like the women who were the first witnesses to Jesus' resurrection, Rhoda has to endure the unbelief and ridicule of others. They concede that it might be Peter's angel at the door. (It was a Jewish custom of the time to believe that each person had an angel who could look like the person and be mistaken for them.) Only when they open the door and see Peter do they believe: 'They were astonished' (v. 16). Only when the disciples saw Jesus did they believe in his resurrection. Does Peter remember that at this point? Do the believers apologize to Rhoda? We don't know.

I often pray for people close to my heart or for things that I wish to happen. I pray for things that I hope will also be on God's heart. But what are my expectations when I pray? Do I expect an answer? Do I recognize the answer when it comes? Do you?

God may choose to do exactly what we ask for—give peace to our worried neighbour, open the heart of our colleague to receive the message of the gospel, heal our sick child, give our church a new direction. He may also choose to answer in a way that we don't expect. His answer might be different from what we had hoped for. It might come through someone who is younger, less experienced, a less mature Christian or even not a Christian at all.

Equally, God can use you or me to bring the answer to someone's prayer, through our words or actions. God is a God of surprises. He might answer our prayers in unexpected ways and he might use unexpected people—like you or me; like Rhoda, the servant girl.

Reflect

- This story also shows that humans, however powerful (like King Herod), cannot stop God's purposes, while the seemingly weak, like Rhoda, can be used by God. Be encouraged!
- Can you think of situations for which you have prayed and where God has surprised you with his answer? Can you think of examples of when God has used you in unexpected ways?
- What are your expectations when you pray?
- You might like to try keeping a prayer diary. Write down one or several things you are praying for today and, after a few weeks, look back to see if you can recognize God's answers, then write them down. This can be immensely encouraging.

✤

Prayer

Lord God, thank you that you are a God who longs to speak to us and listen to us. Give me child-like trust in you to work out your purposes when I pray, and help me to be open to see your answers and to be your answer. Amen.

KRISTINA PETERSEN

LYDIA: LIVING THE LIFE

BIBLE PASSAGE: ACTS 16:11–40

Lydia's childhood home in Thyatira has now been lost beneath its successor Akhisar, in western Turkey, and her adopted Philippi is but a patch of scrubland in northern Greece, littered with ancient rubble. But Lydia, though long since gone to be with her Lord, lives on through his word to encourage and inspire us today.

As a young girl she learnt her craft in that small but successful manufacturing city of Thyatira. Dyeing 'purple' was the primary industry, discarding the small yellow flowers of the madder plant to ferment its red fleshy root. The city's exceptional water quality enhanced the dyeing process, resulting in a depth and consistency of permanent colour held in high regard by affluent clientele.

Whatever Lydia's reasons for sailing to Philippi, it proved a wise decision. Business for 'purple' continued to flourish in this wealthy, luxury-loving colony where the calibre of her fine cloths titillated the lavish tastes of Roman aristocracy. We do not know when she transferred allegiance from her ancestral gods and pagan trade guilds to the God of Israel, but we can indulge our imagination with subsequent events.

How she must have longed for leadership and synagogue fellowship, but that necessitated at least ten men, so once again she made her way out of the city to the customary place of prayer at the riverside grove. Dressed, perhaps, in a linen tunic and purple cloak, her hair piled atop in a golden net, as was the custom of her Roman counterparts, she joined her God-fearing friends.

Greeting one another with loving embrace, they began their

sabbath worship: 'Hear, O Israel: The Lord our God, the Lord is one. Love the Lord your God with all your heart and with all your soul and with all your strength...' (Deuteronomy 6:4–5). But whose were those footsteps approaching? The women arose to greet the newcomers, somewhat hesitant at the arrival of male strangers. Their reserve was unfounded, however, for they too were God-fearers: Paul, Silas, Luke and a younger man called Timothy. Paul spoke to the worshippers of someone called Jesus. As Paul shared his experience while explaining scripture, Lydia immersed herself in the torrent of words washing over her soul as light and truth penetrated her heart. She chewed over Paul's testimony, savoured each text and digested his message with voracious appetite.

Some while later, she startled the servants, bursting through the door in sodden disarray. Alarmed, they scurried around her: had she fallen in the river? Wrapping herself in rugs, she spared no time to change clothes in her enthusiasm to share her newfound faith.

What joy entered the household of Lydia on that fine day! With renewed fervour they sang the sabbath psalm: 'For you make me glad by your deeds, O Lord; I sing for joy at the works of your hands. How great are your works, O Lord, how profound your thoughts!' (Psalm 92:4–5).

Lydia urged the men to stay in her home. There was no argument: they simply could not match her penchant for barter! From the higher-class 'purple' dealer through the middle-class jailer to the lowest of slave girls, the Philippian church—the first in Europe—grew in number, spanning culture, class and profession.

James writes, 'Do not merely listen to the word, and so deceive yourselves. Do what it says' (1:22). Lydia listened to the word of God—that which was already written (our Old Testament) and that being spoken and taught at the time (our New Testament). She acted upon it in faith and continued to live in response to its teaching.

She pursued truth

Would I have listened so intently, or would the gentle breeze in the trees and the river trickling by have distracted my full attention? Not so with Lydia, always hungry for the God she sought in prayer; her anticipation rewarded her.

Stuffy central heating, late nights and hectic activity might tease our mind away from God's message, be it from the pulpit or the still, quiet voice in our personal devotions. Concentration is apt to wander: what is for dinner, what is on TV, what has to be done today?

Proverbs repeatedly encourages us to call out to God for insight, turn our ear to wisdom and apply our mind to understanding, because he has promised, 'Those who seek me find me' (Proverbs 8:17). To 'seek' is not passive but an active pursuit to find something obscured from view. Are we satisfied with a mere belief in God or are we listening intently to hear his voice while seeking him through the Bible, teaching and prayer?

She joined with others to pray

Without a local synagogue, Lydia might have chosen to confine her prayers to the privacy of her home. Community was obviously important to her, however, for on this day of rest she sought out others of like mind, and so they established that 'place of prayer' (Acts 16:13).

What importance do you place upon corporate prayer? From the doubts of Thomas to the power of Pentecost, from the miraculous release of imprisoned Peter to the faith-inspired word by the riverside, the Acts of the Apostles would have been so very different if the believers had not met for prayer.

What do we miss out on when we fail to meet together: faith, peace, power, release, insight, revelation, teaching and encouragement? 'Let us not give up meeting together... but let us encourage one another' (Hebrews 10:25).

She set priorities

Lydia controlled her business affairs; they did not control her. She knew how to keep them in their rightful place and was not afraid to do so, even in a culture in which the majority—all but a few women, in fact—did not respect God's holy day.

Jesus freed us from the religious observance of a sabbath bound by human rules and regulations, but reminds us that a day of rest was instigated for our physical and spiritual well-being (Mark 2:27). The fourth commandment was a blessing from God, so that men and women and their animals would rest from their labours, and in so doing find time for refreshment in him. Lydia honoured God above her livelihood—no small thing in days when single women were prone to poverty—and how God blessed her, her household and the ongoing success of her business!

What are our priorities? Do we prioritize a day of rest each week, or is it used to catch up with housework, shopping, overtime, and so on? Juggling my responsibilities as mother, minister's wife, administrator, church member, volunteer and writer, my chosen rest day could so easily become a catch-up day. But I hear God's voice even as I write, calling me to 'catch up' with him. Who is the boss? Whom do we fear more? 'Fear of man will prove to be a snare, but whoever trusts in the Lord is kept safe' (Proverbs 29:25).

She promptly obeyed

Lydia and all her household were baptized. It was not forced upon them but was their choice in response to God's challenge.

What is the Lord asking of you today: to share your testimony in your home, at work, with friends, or neighbours; to be baptized; to turn away from old habits or traditions; to embrace something new? Whatever he lays on your heart, do not delay, for tomorrow may be too late.

She served whole-heartedly

Lydia not only asked, she urged and persuaded the apostles to partake of her generous hospitality. Her initial token of gratitude conceived and subsequently gave birth to the Philippian church, who in turn raised gifts to support God's work elsewhere (Philippians 4:14–19).

Despite what was quite probably a comfortable, spacious home, I have no doubt that the offer inconvenienced her, for she was a busy, successful trader, but serving God took precedence and she did not excuse herself.

Hospitality—sharing what we have with others—is a require-ment of Christian love in practice (Romans 12:13; 1 Peter 4:9). As we are generous with all that we have, to refresh, care and provide for the needs of others, we shall also touch Jesus, for whatever we do for the least of our brothers and sisters, we do for him (Matthew 25:40).

Lydia emulates Romans 12:11: 'Never be lacking in zeal, but keep your spiritual fervour, serving the Lord.' In response to God's message, she did what she could do, using what and who she knew and all that she owned.

What resources and abilities has God given to you, and are you using them? Continue to grow in your relationship with the Lord through actively seeking him in his word and in prayer, balanced with whole-hearted service. Listen to his specific command for your life and do what he says.

Reflect

- *Lydia the craftswoman:* Are you gifted with your hands? Joining or starting up a craft or sewing group is a tremendous opportunity to share your testimony and God's love with non-believing friends, as you earn their trust over weeks of working together in a relaxed and mutually enjoyable environment. Furthermore, the goods you make might be sold to raise funds for missionaries or charitable causes.
- *Lydia the intellectual:* Do you like to stimulate thought as you engage with God's word? Perhaps you can share some of your findings at midweek meetings or home groups or by talking with non-Christian friends.
- *Lydia the homemaker:* You do not need to have a spacious, wealthy home to be hospitable. Whether it's a cup of coffee, a simple meal or an overnight stop, God can use your home and love to encourage the needy, care for the convalescent and provide for the travelling preacher or missionary on furlough. If you have room, groups for Alpha, Activate and other evangelism initiatives could also take place under your roof.
- *Lydia the businesswoman:* Are you gifted with business acumen and money-making skills? You may be the only Christian your colleagues know: your integrity will influence and your testimony challenge them while your income blesses those to whom God sends it.
- *Lydia the time-giver:* Time is a precious commodity these days, and yet we all share the same 24 hours each day. The question is how we choose to fill them. Is our time given to God or kept for ourselves? Are we willing to sacrifice it in order to help people who need our friendship, practical support and prayer?

✣

Prayer

Join me in prayer with King David: 'Teach me your way, O Lord, and I will walk in your truth; give me an undivided heart, that I may fear your name' (Psalm 86:11).

ANNE LE TISSIER

(EXTRA)ORDINARY WOMEN

Reflections for women on Bible-based living

Clare Blake

Have you ever felt that women in the Bible were superstars, somehow extra specially blessed by God? And then looked at yourself...?

This book of down-to-earth Bible reflections is based around the central theme that all women are special in God's eyes. Relating scripture teaching to everyday experience, it shows how God has a special gifting for each of us, how we can turn to him when life doesn't make sense, and how to set about discovering his will for our lives.

Taking a fresh look at the stories of Sarah, Leah, Mary and other Bible characters, we see how God looks beyond our failures and weaknesses to the women he has created us to be as we learn to follow him, step by step.

To him, each one of us is a 'one off' and in his eyes there are no 'ordinary' women—only 'extraordinary' women.

ISBN 1 84101 235 1   £6.99
Available from your local Christian bookshop or, in case of difficulty, direct from BRF using the order form on page 96.

★ Also from BRF ★

QUIET SPACES

Prayer interludes for busy women

Patricia Wilson

The intimate relationship with God you've yearned for is well within your grasp, despite the chaos of juggling multiple roles, deadlines, and commitments. This book can help you to use even a few stray minutes as an opportunity for a 'prayer interlude', calming the mind and listening for God's still, small voice in the midst of the tumult around you.

Each 'prayer interlude', which can be completed in as little as five minutes, offers a calming passage from the Psalms, a prayer meditation, a thought from the words of Jesus, and an exercise to help readers as they go back into the busyness of the day.

ISBN 1 84101 339 0   £5.99
Available from your local Christian bookshop or, in case of difficulty, direct from BRF using the order form on page 96.

CHANGING LIVES!

Daily readings for women who want more than a makeover

Edited by Catherine Butcher

If God is the Great Designer, what are his plans for our lives? In *Changing Lives!* some of today's best Christian women writers look into the Bible to discover how God works to transform our everyday lives.

These thoughts and insights by women for women were originally contributed to *Day by Day with God*. Now they are brought together in four sections, starting with a focus on Jesus—the one worth following.

As well as a short reading and a prayer or point for reflection, the writers show their practical understanding of the Bible and deep empathy with readers through their comments and anecdotes, which bring scripture to life.

ISBN 1 84101 419 2   £9.99
Available from your local Christian bookshop or, in case of difficulty, direct from BRF using the order form on page 96.

DAY BY DAY WITH GOD

Rooting women's lives in the Bible

Edited by Catherine Butcher

Treat yourself to time out with God every day! Published three times a year, in January, May and September, *Day by Day with God* provides a short printed Bible passage, explained and applied especially for women, by women who have themselves found the Bible a source of strength and inspiration for life. A suggested daily prayer or meditation, plus further reading to explore, will help you connect the daily notes with your own spiritual journey as you seek to follow Jesus more closely.

Anne Le Tissier and Kristina Petersen are both on the team of contributors to *Day by Day with God*, which can be obtained from your local Christian bookshop or by subscription direct from BRF.

BRF
First Floor, Elsfield Hall
15–17 Elsfield Way
Oxford
OX2 8FG

Tel: 01865 319700
Fax: 01865 319701
E-mail: subscriptions@brf.org.uk
Website: www.brf.org.uk

ORDER FORM

REF	TITLE	PRICE	QTY	TOTAL
235 1	*(Extra)Ordinary Women*	£6.99		
339 0	*Quiet Spaces*	£5.99		
419 2	*Changing Lives!*	£9.99		

POSTAGE AND PACKING CHARGES					
order value	UK	Europe	Surface	Air Mail	Postage and packing:
£7.00 & under	£1.25	£3.00	£3.50	£5.50	Donation:
£7.01–£30.00	£2.25	£5.50	£6.50	£10.00	**Total enclosed:**
Over £30.00	free	prices on request			

Name _____ Account Number _____

Address_____

_____ Postcode _____

Telephone Number _____ Email _____

Payment by: Cheque ❑ Mastercard ❑ Visa ❑ Postal Order ❑ Switch ❑

Credit card no. ☐☐☐☐ ☐☐☐☐ ☐☐☐☐ ☐☐☐☐ Expires ☐☐ ☐☐

Switch card no. ☐☐☐☐☐☐☐☐☐☐☐☐☐☐☐☐☐☐

Issue no. of Switch card ☐☐☐☐ Expires ☐☐ ☐☐

Signature _____ Date _____

All orders must be accompanied by the appropriate payment.

Please send your completed order form to:
BRF, First Floor, Elsfield Hall, 15–17 Elsfield Way, Oxford OX2 8FG
Tel. 01865 319700 / Fax. 01865 319701 Email: enquiries@brf.org.uk

❑ Please send me further information about BRF publications.

Available from your local Christian bookshop. 　　　　　　　BRF is a Registered Charity